The mystery of death- ... ages—has now beei ... (- throughs" revealed in ***Life*** ... quent books, *near death ex* ... e back" in images as wild and baffling as anything in the movies.

Predictably, as powerful digital special effects have rapidly advanced, movies such as the academy award winning film ***The Sixth Sense*** and ***What Dreams May Come*** have been able to convincingly portray the latest paradigms of the afterlife. These and other films show digitally enhanced scenes of the deathplane, beings-of-light, disembodied spirits, souls in an intermediate plane awaiting rebirth, astral planes, psychic contacts to and from the other side, non-human entities, astral travel, mediums, channeling, earthbound spirits, as well as a host of other things—all previously described in an array of bestselling books and now a cornerstone of New Age thought.

Those with the most celebrated "near death experiences" have gone on to become media superstars, selling millions of books while appearing on prime-time television. A whole new related category of mediumistic psychics, able to perform spirit readings on demand, have appeared before live television audiences to further feed the public's appetite.

But is this new paradigm of the afterlife what really happens at death? Or are such *experiences*—and that's the key—a spiritual cocktail for a modern age that has been adrift and perplexed? Is it a symptom of a culture that has lost its spiritual roots and is desperate to embrace what turns out to be one of the oldest occult terrain in history?

A credible and unique source claims that this supposedly new paradigm is a dangerous deception spanning back to the ancient mediums of Babylon and Chaldea when Saul sought the Witch of Endor.

The Mystery of Death contends that there are realities that need to be considered in order to get the full picture. At stake is what happens to the human soul whose worth is beyond measure.

Tal Brooke is the President/Chairman of Spiritual Counterfeits Project (SCP, Inc., www.scp-inc.org), a Berkeley-based research organization. He has authored eight books and his work has been recognized in Marquis *Who's Who in the World*, *Contemporary Authors* (Vol. 93-96), and *The International Who's Who of Authors*. He received an EPA first place award in the critical review category. A graduate of the University of Virginia and Princeton, Tal Brooke has spoken at Cambridge, Oxford, Princeton, Sorbonne, U.C. Berkeley, the University of Virginia, and the University of Edinburgh.

Other books by Tal Brooke:

One World, millennial edition (When the World...)

Avatar of Night, the millennial edition

Riders of The Cosmic Circuit (iuniverse.com)

Virtual Gods

Conspiracy to Silence the Son of God

When The World Will Be As One

The Other Side of Death

End Run Publishing
1442A Walnut St., #387
Berkeley, CA, 94709
Order Dept: 800-266-5564

First End Run Edition August 2001

Cover preparation & design by Brian Godawa & Tal Brooke

Photos by Tal Brooke, including: public domain, royalty free, reviewer photos, Corel series, photobank, Corbis, softkey, etc.

Graphics by Tal Brooke, Frank Ordaz & Brian Godawa

Manufactured in the United States of America

ISBN:1-930045-05-0

THE MYSTERY OF DEATH

Special Millennial Edition of

THE OTHER SIDE OF DEATH

Tal Brooke

an End Run Book

Contents

1

An Overview

In the past few decades, the mystery of death has been apparently solved by a new category of "scientific breakthroughs" in the realm of advanced resuscitation methods in medical technology. Those declared "clinically dead" have apparently come back with a wide range of reports about the afterlife. Some of these reports, as in the case of Betty Eadie, have become mega-bestsellers. Researchers—and at the head of the pack is Dr. Raymond Moody—go on to interpret the ultimate meaning of these near death reports. Each researcher peering into this garbled field of death reports ends up reading into the "data" their own schema of afterlife. Meanwhile, those who underwent the "near death experience" often become spiritual teachers and media celebrities to the public at large. The movie, *What Dreams May Come*, starring Robin Williams, is a pastiche of these afterlife reports.

Yet often, the "data" that the experts have grasped to prove their beliefs—all based on testimonies of *experience*—can, like Proteus, change in an instant, turn, and ultimately destroy the faith that sought to use it.

The argument in essence amounts to this: If you believe in one report you are forced to believe them all, and then you are left to tabulate them through a sort of voting system with majority rule. Meanwhile, no one ever seems to bring up the problem of *deception*.

A spiritualist, whose cause is the easiest to "prove," simply says, "See, any of these reports proves that there is an afterlife." A liberal Christian claims, "Yes, and all twenty of my subjects said that they saw heaven." Then an orthodox Christian claims in rebuttal, "Ah, yes, but what you don't realize is that I have resuscitated thirty people who saw hell." But the death blow is apparently delivered to the orthodox Christian when the Hindu Vedantist comes along and claims, "Not all of your beings-of-light were this Christ being; five of our international subjects reported Krishna, two saw Buddha, and we found any number of ascended masters. Besides, there are variant realms of death planes, not just heaven and hell."

Even if the orthodox Christian drums up ten thousand cases that support his belief, just a handful of exceptions blows his watertight argument.

It is a trap. To allow experience to be the sole arbiter of truth makes you supremely vulnerable to deception.

The Christians have rushed headlong into this maze, naively oblivious to the bottleneck farther along the way that will trap them. But I there is an entire range of knowledge that has been almost totally omitted in previous attempts to untangle this mystery of "clinical death" reports. And with this, a wholly new pattern has emerged which clarifies the puzzle.

Several different approaches to understanding death are prevalent in the world today. In one tradition, mystics, gurus, and mediums claim the authority of firsthand experience.

Then there is the scientific approach whereby the experts attempt to somehow rationally and experimentally understand life and death. In the philosophical approach, academics use the intellect alone to reason out and philosophize the meanings of life, death, and existence.

The final category, is about the biblical tradition, which provides for the possibility of the very God of the universe revealing the truths of existence, life, death, and himself through self-revelation.

The categories mentioned above fit into three major traditions: the biblical tradition, the Western tradition, and the Eastern or ancient tradition.

Since the Eastern tradition can be traced back to the ancient mystery religions, it is sometimes referred to as "the ancient tradition." The modern phenomena of the psychics are in the lineage of the ancient tradition, because they are not modern at all; their roots are ancient. Psychics appeared in ancient Egypt, Chaldea, Persia, Babylon, Greece, and India. The psychics

and mediums were the very oracles of Babylon and ancient Greece.

Indeed, the psychics boast of having the oldest access to the secrets and realities behind the mystery of death. They have permeated many cultures, though Babylon was the most famous. Now they have gained a very prominent voice here in the West. Books by and about a number of famous psychics and mediums are best sellers. Societies have been founded in their names, such as Edgar Cayce's Association for Research and Enlightenment (A.R.E.), Arthur Ford's Spiritual Frontiers Fellowship, The Theosophists, The Rosicrucians, the Masons, and The Brotherhood of the Seven Rays.

Psychics have been included within the inner circles of numerous governments, from Franklin D. Roosevelt's presidency to Hitler's Third Reich. TV specials show psychics in action, such as Uri Geller bending a knife merely by staring at it, Peter Hurkos solving the Boston Strangler murders, or Ted Serios staring down the lens of a camera and mentally projecting an image on unexposed film. Almost all of these psychics claim to be in touch with beings "on the other side." Geller has claimed that he does not receive his powers from any hidden source within his mind, but directly through beings with whom he is in contact, who channel their powers through him. Meanwhile, James Van Praagh, on prime-time TV, claims to talk to the invisible dead relatives of his audience.

Doctor Raymond Moody, a medical doctor as well as a Ph.D. of philosophy, mentions that many of his subjects who "returned from death" have become psychic. Indeed, the common pattern of his subjects fits most readily into the pattern of psychic experience and mediumistic contacts with the beyond. Perhaps this is why Dr. Elizabeth Kubler-Ross, a psychiatrist and an associate of Moody's, confessed her use of mediums as primary source material. She found that the mediums contacted the same sources that her subjects did.

In essence, psychics and mediums claim that they can pass into the spirit world, or the realm of the dead, with as much ease as a person can walk through a door to get to another room. They claim that this realm is really another dimension, invisible in form, which intersects our physical universe. They assert that the inner spirit within them has access to both the physical dimension of everyday life and the spiritual dimension of deceased people and other types of beings.

For a psychic to pass through this doorway, he must "enter the deep unconscious realm of his spirit," become oblivious to this world, and commune with the other world in a trance—the link between both worlds. The body of knowledge that psychics and mediums have claimed to have amassed across the ages is either from their entering this realm in a "spirit body" or through contact teachings from departed spirits or higher spiritual beings. A familiar term for these higher beings is "being of light."

Let me confess that as a child I had a kind of psychic obsession that led me to seek out numerous psychic experiences such as clairvoyance, telepathy, out-of-the-body experiences, and sensitivity to "spirits."

Perhaps the main door opened when I obtained a Ouija board when I was ten. Soon after I felt "presences" in my room at night. Our London housemaid, who also worked for a famous medium, answered my endless questions about the spirit realm and modern spiritualism, feeding a growing curiosity like a line of crumbs.

Years later, after going to India, I learned where this line of crumbs led. What at first seemed enthralling, fascinating, often frightening and mystifying took a dark turn. In India I saw that the trail of crumbs led over an abyss and the biblical warnings about trafficking in the occult suddenly made sense. I had finally run head-long into dark spiritual powers in India. I also learned about the reality spiritual deception—a high stakes game given the value of the human soul.

It is time to bring into honest question some of the abundant enthusiasm today's psychics and researchers have impressed on the public in their present proselytizings of the "near death experience" and the occult belief system lurking behind it.

We are going to use an "open the case" courtroom approach, occasionally pitting today's statements coming out of a host of near death experiences against the biblical tradition. Surely if there is true unity, it will become abundantly clear; if not, that, too, will clear the air.

The timeless mystery of death and what happens after we die is too important to ignore or down play. And if there really is such a thing as deception in the spiritual arena, we need to know it. We definitely need to make sense of all the recent near-death reports. Too much is at stake not to go on this quest for the truth.

2

Crossing the Other Side

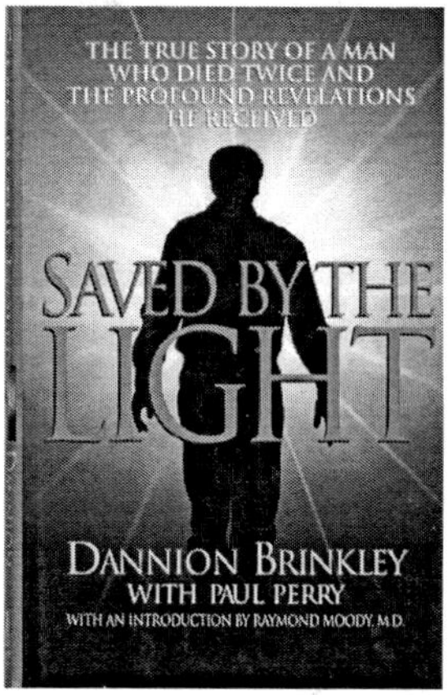

Increasing numbers are reporting having died and come back, altered states of consciousness or contacts from beyond with beings of light, cosmic masters, channeled entities, gods, or even "God" appearing in a new form. The elite of these are soon discovered by the media.

What was once faint crackling on America's spiritual Geiger counter has become deafening noise as these messages about the afterlife come in like cosmic telegrams. They often bear the delicious promise that the human race will transform into an exalted godlike state that will bring in the New Age. But standing in the way of this necessary paradigm shift are the old "prejudices" and beliefs from an outmoded Christian era with its dualistic view of God and man, its moral absolutes of good and evil.

The reigning books on the *New York Times* bestseller list for well over a decade have been books about contacting the other side or experiencing new realities. Betty Eadie's 1992 *Embraced By the Light* by mid 1994 had reached the 66-week mark on the *New York Times* best seller list, primarily holding the number one spot. Then Dannion Brinkley's

1994 *Saved By the Light* got to the top position and toggled between one and two with Eadie's book. By early 1998, James Van Praagh published the bestselling account of his own contact with the other side entitled, *Talking To Heaven: A Medium's Message of Life After Death*, which took over the *New York Times* pole position. Van Praagh was on Oprah Winfrey, Larry King, and *Good Morning America* following the footsteps of Eadie and Brinkley. A little after, Gary Zukav and Neal Donald Walsch entered the stream of media celebrity along with Marianne Williamson, Deepak Chopra, and James Redfield.

These best selling authors have been invading the nation's imagination with their experiences and revelations, creating a psychic and paranormal "Great Awakening."

With these contacts have come messages, and this is the real heart of the matter. What is interesting is that these messages have woven together to form an interesting pattern—indeed, a belief system. The synchronicity of these messages and their divergent points of contact keep suggesting that at least some of these communications are most deliberate and that something is being orchestrated from beyond our known world.

But for what reason? And why is it happening now at an accelerating pace? It did not happen overnight; it has been building up for centuries. Why now? And is there a supernatural dimension to the geopolitical plan?

These messages constantly bring teachings about the New Age and world community. Who can resist such messages, especially when they come from near death experiences?

The Near Death Experience

. . . You watch in awe as a tunnel of darkness suddenly appears before you. In moments it is ready to engulf you. You go flashing down the tunnel at tremendous speed as a brilliant light at the end grows larger and larger. At the end of the tunnel stands a Being of Light. You are about to be shown a "life review" by this being of light who seems to know you through and through.

You have entered the Death plane.

Then you glide above a vast jeweled city filled with bright and luminous "wise beings" who can now talk to you telepathically. They have a message that they want you to convey to the rest of the world. You descend to some vast courtyard surrounded by pillars reminiscent of the Parthenon. Standing before them, these beings show you the earth's future, a time of coming changes when luminous masters, world helpers, will guide the earth through upheavals into a time of world peace and harmony.

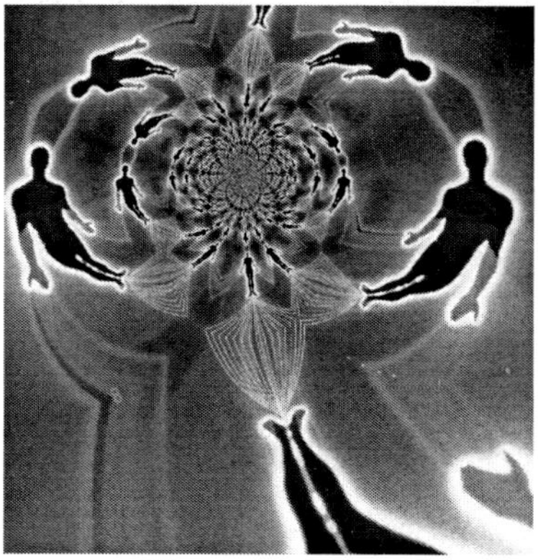

Suddenly, you realize that billions across history have crossed this threshold. Only up until now, this has been a shrouded secret, one that could have remained sealed forever. Soon this glistening region retreats from view.

You hover between "clinical death" and resuscitation during this "near death experience." As you come back into the world, crossing the threshold of heavy matter, you enter your lifeless body as it lies on a stretcher. Your "astral body" descends into it like a hand plunging into a glove. In the process you invisibly pass by physicians and orderlies working frantically to bring your body back to life. According to modern instruments, you were dead, and all vital signs had ceased.

You have returned from the dead. When you open your eyes, those nearby look on dumbstruck. You are both sad and grateful to have more time on earth.

You the viewer have been watching the televised account of a now famous figure who has had a "death experience." Special effects reminiscent of Star Wars have turbocharged the television portrayal of what lies behind the mystery of death. You relive what happened through the eyes of the subject. It is powerful, real, and immediate, and because you have been made to identify with the dying subject, you also sympathize with the account.

In truth, program is the pinnacle of media endorsement—a lavish prime-time special on major network television that is exclusively devoted to the amazing account of a death experience. This televised account is actually a composite of two famous accounts—that of Betty Eadie, and Dannion Brinkley. Their separate accounts have also been recreated on prime time network specials since the generic "synthesis" just watched.

Dannion Brinkley had his near death experience when hit by a bolt of lightening. Recovery was long and agonizing, but this former troublemaker had a tale to tell from his higher masters and spirit guides. His account is one of future glimpses of a unified world and messages from the Wise Beings. Christ does not really fit the picture. With Eadie, Christ is portrayed as a being of light.

Betty Eadie had her experience after she decided, after a "multitude of problems" following the birth of a seventh child, to have a hysterectomy. It was performed on November 18, 1973, at Riverton hospital (now Highline Specialty Center) in Seattle, Washington.

Eadie recalls being given sleeping pills before and after the surgery, making her "groggy." In this groggy state, she remembers noticing it was 9:30 p. m. before she fell back asleep "chilled and weaker than I had ever felt before."

She claims to have died for over four hours. How does one know? Were there any doctors, nurses, or anyone in the room during these hours? No, because when she revived, there was still no one in the room (except demons and angels). There was no sheet over her face.

The only way she knows that she died is because during her experience she claims Jesus told her she had died—prematurely. Medical records are sketchy, and to this day she refuses to release them.

She soon takes the reader on a vivid recollection of a journey out of her body into heaven. She describes in detail her many encounters with Jesus, old friends from her preexistence, ministering angels, and other beings.

The content of this experience is filled with mixtures of historic Biblical Christianity, Mormonism, New Age philosophy, occultism, and Catholicism. Especially prevalent are the trappings and direct teachings of folk Mormonism and official LDS doctrine.

Upon "leaving her body," Eadie was met by three men curiously dressed in traditional Catholic monk's robes. They had been with her for "eternities." Eadie begins to recall images of her preexistence, her pre-earth life, recognizing old spirit being acquaintances, and that her "death" was a rebirth to greater understanding and knowledge (Eadie, pp. 31, 34-35, 68, 73, 82, 97, 100).

Eadie communicates with her "ministering angels" through something more than "telepathy." She claimed to be able to feel "their emotions and . . . experience their feelings" (p. 32). This was the beginning of several allusions to an undifferentiated oneness of eternal intelligence, of all things (pp. 31, 55, 57, 76, 79, 81, 87, 93). This is the Eastern spin.

Eadie claims that every particle, every element comprising matter has spirit and an eternal intelligence. Later while in a garden in Heaven, Eadie claims to have seen a rose and could "feel its spirit. . . such intelligence within that petal. . . I felt God in the plant, in me, his love pouring into us. **We are all one"** (pp. 79-81). Since her first book, this account has evolved and her teachings have drifted toward some of the Earth Consciousness of her native American ancestry.

From New Age groups to church groups, eager readers circulate Betty Eadie's book basking in the gushing positive affirmations from the other side. It is a picture of a universe so tender and mild that you could almost wander around blindfolded and never so much as trip. (Try doing the same thing in the real world in a Detroit ghetto or Harlem.). That's the thing about Eadie's message, she gushes and it's all good. It is like she found a massive Oreo Cookie for the world. The same can be said for now deceased New Age channeler, Helen Schucman, who channeled *A Course in Miracles* from some cosmic Christ-spirit. It all sounds far too good to be true.

As we shall see later, not every near death survivor nor every medium has such a positive report. Some channelers go into a danger zone that has clear warning signs—warnings that all may not be well. Some reports tell you that you have to absorb both the good and the evil because they are all one.

3

The New Breakthrough

The mystery of death gripped me even when I was a small child. It was something no one was free from, and it could spring unannounced upon almost anybody, carrying the force of some mystical tornado. I sensed that if anybody could figure out where it led, he would have a profound handle on ultimate truth. The invention of all time would be the discovery that could bring back the dead. One Sunday morning when I was nine years old, I remember pining wistfully over the news picture of a pretty girl who had died during an epileptic attack. Though I did not know her, I felt overwhelming loss. In a sense it was the ultimate indignity, but no amount of thought could penetrate the dense cloud of unknowing. The authorities of the adult world around me were at a loss for explanation.

Then when I was twelve years old—two years after getting the Ouija board—I stood at a book rack and discovered *The Case for Bridey Murphy.* I learned a new word: *reincarnation.* The book unfolded the amazing story of Bridey Murphy going from regressive hypnosis across the great divide to a previous life as a girl in Ireland. It was incredible. It occurred to me that if even one case could be substantiated, my view of life would be changed radically. It meant that I was old, for the age of our bodies was irrelevant to our spiritual age. If we reincarnated even once, who could limit the number of times it might happen? I felt a sense of relief.

Then, later, other things became linked with the Bridey Murphy scheme as I began to read a popular parapsychic journal, Fate Magazine. Maybe ghosts were spirits caught between incarnations.

When I was fifteen, another door was pried open. A friend of mine had a tonsillectomy. After the operation at a hospital in Beirut, Lebanon, he was left with a most peculiar and vivid memory. He had left his body for a time. Shooting out in an exuberant rush of energy, he had soared up into a stratosphere of sublime hues as the pandemonium below vanished almost out of sight. The "cord" leading to his body would only let him go so high—to the edge of the earth's barrier. But there he met a spirit that said he had been killed in Korea. Just then, my friend was yanked back inside his body. For days we both jubilated over his experience.

Sporadically, over the next ten years, other pieces of the puzzle fell into place, finally forming a picture of death almost identical to what recent thanatologists like Dr. Raymond Moody have proclaimed. Edgar Cayce, a psychic in Virginia Beach, Virginia, had said a lot about it, and a few massive doses of LSD sealed it off for me, until I walked around in such a closed bottle of spiritual certainty that proof to the contrary would have barely dented my wall of beliefs. On the other hand, if a scientist had appeared with evidence backing up my beliefs, I would have seized it with joy. I was infatuated with my new sense of spiritual freedom.

What I did not realize was that my view of death fit into a tradition that was only one option among a handful of traditions; my view was molded from ideas that had filtered from the East, and its root in history went back to ancient India, Babylon, Chaldea, and Egypt. What I failed to consider was that another great tradition existed whose alternative, equally weighty, was not necessarily in accord with what I believed. What the world needed was a scientist to supply proof which would settle the debate between the great traditions, once and for all.

Pioneers of the Near Death Experience

Medical doctors Raymond Moody and Elizabeth Kubler-Ross made their debut over 20 years ago, appearing to be those scientists for whom I might have hoped, and the world eagerly devoured their discoveries, which seem so appropriate for our age. Their discoveries are "based on experiences," or at least internal experiences; and though they cannot be controlled by using the laboratory method, they appear to be phenomena, though they are not directly observable. Still, one wonders what is really new. Throughout history various persons have claimed to have had certain types of experiences as visionaries, mystics, people in the saucer cults, and so on. What needed to be settled was the issue of ultimate reality, not different categories of private experience. Either God was or was not. Then, if he did exist, what was his true nature? By this we would learn that some experiences were real, while others were more like hallucinations or mirages. What was needed was a reliable criterion. Science has seemed to be the answer, though it is a self-limiting field by definition.

How objective is the scientist? Moody, in the introduction to *Life After Life*, submits that his book, "written as it is by a human being, naturally reflects the background, opinions and prejudices of its author."[1] That is true; I knew Moody quite well in college and can vouch for our mutual interest in the more mystical interpretation of existence, for we both speculated about reincarnation and related subjects. Our mutual friend, George Ritchie, in his own death experience taught that reincarnation was a definite reality, and that what many of the Eastern mystics taught was a reality which fit into a more liberal picture of "Christ consciousness."

The gist of *Life After Life* is that beneath the neat scientific reporting is a distinct framework of reality which draws upon the testimony of fifty "clinical deaths" to yoke, by implication, the world religions by analogy. Moody maintains that there is a link, if you use a certain slant, between Hinduism, Buddhism, and Christianity in their teachings about death, and that after death the soul lives on (which apparently agrees with all religions), evolves (love and knowledge being the spiritual universals sought), and very possibly reincarnates. As Kubler-Ross would contend, we begin to see death and its workings in the universe as a laboratory for spiritual evolution. At the end of his book, Moody clearly states that his work does not constitute any sort of proof by scientific criteria. Rather, it all seems to be in a strange new category of its own, a modern enigma that touches science and religion, which perhaps has only been possible with the advent of sophisticated medical equipment that can "keep the dead from dying" or revive those thought dead.

The heart of Moody's discovery is the following model of what happens at death, an ideal composite of fifteen elements which have a high statistical occurrence among his subjects, though no case had all fifteen and only a few had twelve or more:

> A man is dying and, as he reaches the point of greatest physical distress, he hears himself pronounced dead by his doctor. He begins to hear an uncomfortable noise, a loud ringing or buzzing, and at the same time feels himself moving very rapidly through a long dark tunnel. After this, he suddenly finds himself outside his own physical body, but still in the immediate physical environment, and sees his own body from a distance, as though he is a spectator. He watches the resuscitation attempt from this unusual vantage point and is in a state of emotional upheaval.
>
> After a while, he collects himself and becomes more accustomed to his odd condition. He notices that he still has a "body," but one of a very different nature and with very different powers from the physical body he has left behind. Soon other things begin to happen. Others come to meet and to help him. He glimpses the spirits of relatives and friends who have already died, and a loving, warm spirit of a kind he has never encountered before—a being of light—appears before him. This being asks him a question, non verbally, to make him evaluate his life and helps him along by showing him a panoramic, instantaneous playback of the major events of his life. At some point he finds himself approaching some sort of barrier or border, apparently representing the limit between earthly life and the next life. Yet, he finds that he must go back to the earth, that the time for his death has not yet come. At this point he resists, for by now he is taken up with his experiences in the afterlife and does not want to return. He is overwhelmed by intense feelings of joy, love, and peace. Despite his attitude, though, he somehow reunites with his physical body and lives.[2]

Moody goes on to describe, in the course of his book, how the recovered subject goes out into a truth-rejecting world which forces him to conceal what he knows. As was true in past history, we learn that there will be a certain amount of witch hunting before the world becomes acclimated enough to the truth to accept it.

How are we to understand these baffling phenomena in a materialistic world which makes no provision for such things? The answer is given in Moody's chapter entitled "Parallels." This is where the syncretism of the world religions occurs, but it takes a certain slant to succeed. Part of the slant is a theological error. The Bible, according to Moody, "has relatively little to say about the events that transpire upon death, or about the precise nature of the after-death."[3] Then he cites several passages which in an oblique way appear to relate to his discoveries (out-of-body experiences and beings of light). In the mysticism of Plato and Emanuel Swedenborg, the parallel sticks; but when Moody mentions the secret teachings in *The Tibetan Book of the Dead*, the kernel of his discoveries is fully described and endorsed by no less than Eastern mystics scores of centuries before our modern age. That is a potent clue to who has the answer. Moody says, "The correspondence between the early stages of death which it [The *Tibetan Book of* the Dead] relates and those which have been recounted to me by those who have come near to death is nothing short of fantastic."[4] The Tibetan book, however, goes on to describe further phases of the death journey which Moody's subjects were unable to reach: realms of souls, planes of being, hell worlds, paradise planes, illuminated gods, and the secrets of transmigration. The thing to do, if this is the case, is to seek those Tibetans who have experienced the complete death journey. (This is what 1 did in 1969 when I went to India and studied under the yogis, as

Bardo Thodol—The Tibetan Book of the Dead

anyone who is serious about pursuing this subject would do.)

If *The Tibetan Book of the Dead* has been sitting quietly with all the secrets which we in the West have missed, this opens the doors to its brother and sister books of India, such as *The Upanishads*, *The Srimad Bhagavata*, *The Bhagavad Gita*, *The Puranas*, *Vedas*, *Sutras*, and *Ramayana*. If that door opens, the writings of the yogis have to be fair game. One's authority must become the writings of Ramanah Maharishi, Yogananda, Meher Baba, Vivekananda, Sri Aurobindo, Ramakrishna, Patanjali, and Shankaracharya.

What does Shankaracharya teach, for instance? That the primary stage of learning comes when the aspirant dissociates his "self" from his physical body. "You are not your body." In fact, the body is to be mentally discarded (the path of Varaigya), for it is only transient and hence illusory. This is step one toward the mystical philosophy implied in Moody's documentation of consciousness as an entity apart from the body, where release is a "relief."

Step two toward mystical philosophy in Moody's findings is the possibility of reincarnation, which he leaves open. He suggests we read Ian Stevenson's *Twenty* Cases *Suggestive of Reincarnation.* (Dr. Stevenson, who was formerly on the faculty at the University of Virginia, where we were, was an associate of Dr. Ritchie.) Reincarnation is a mechanism of "soul evolution" in Hinduism and pantheism. It is through various bodies that the self reaches identity or becomes one with the godhead.

Step three toward Eastern religion in Moody's scheme is the "being of light." Time and again in the writings of the yogis, their deceased masters visit them in the form of a being of light. Other times, different gods visit them as forms of light (*Jyothir Murthi*, "god-form of light"). Sri Yukteshwar and Lahiri Mahasaya both visited Parmahamsa Yogananda from the astral plane as masters of light, and Ramakrishna saw his goddess, Kali, as a brilliant being of light. Kubler-Ross has a spirit guide too.

Step four in Moody's discoveries is the new (really *old)* view of good and evil. The Hindus view good and evil as illusions. Indeed, all pairs of opposites are unresolved illusions which can only be dissolved in the "oneness of the universe." If it is all one, good and evil are ultimately joined. The Hindus define "evil" ultimately as ignorance or any obstacle in the path of evolution. In case after case of astral encounter, the subject testifies that the being of light did not judge or condemn, but merely exuded great love and warmth, bringing the subject to a deeper knowledge of himself in which good and evil became subservient to his evolutionary needs. Evil comes to mean that the subject has not grown sufficiently or has not "loved" enough. Good and evil, therefore, are not distinctively antithetical and absolute qualities of which the Bible speaks. To get beyond the "primitive" idea of absolute good and evil is an evolutionary technique, basic to all forms of yoga and mystical thought. Interestingly, it is also promulgated by the Satantists (Aleister Crowley, Anton LaVey, Sybil Leek) and psychic mediums (Jane Roberts, Arthur Ford, etc.).

How does the being of light deal with the problem of evil? It is a being of liberal, "loving" permissiveness that counters our sins with "good vibrations." On the "other side," there is not so much punishment as there is cause-and-effect feedback for the higher good of the soul. Sin against others is minimized, often in jocular humor, which the being of light often engages in when reviewing the subject's life. Not even a whisper of a mention is made about sin against God (a root biblical concept).

When I picked up the Bridey Murphy book as a young boy, I did not realize that since history's beginning a distinct antithesis or warring has existed between two major traditions of thought and spirituality. Two alternatives of perspective (one perilous) were in the Garden of Eden. When ancient Israel was once chosen by God as a nation, there was the Chaldean-Babylonian religious system, which the God of the Jews opposed, forbidding his people to have any dealings with their religious "abominations." God told them of the differences which separated the living God of Moses from the secret mysteries of the Babylonians. Israel and Babylon represent the perennial struggle between the direct, exoteric, universal, and absolute revelation of God sovereignly intervening in history, as opposed to the occult, esoteric, Gnostic mysteries of a man-based mystical pursuit of self evolution (even to the point of merging with God). Their views of death contrast as sharply as all their other areas of disagreement, as we shall see. Consider, for example, that the crowning lie of the adversary, through the serpent, was the proclamation to Eve, "Ye shall not surely die" (Gen. 3:4).

In Revelation, the last book of the Bible, is a prediction about a future worldwide reappearance of Babylon, with all its ancient mysteries, reigning as the religion of the world. Called "Mystery Babylon," it is ingenious, so clever in its metaphysical system of counterfeit spiritual truths that it seduces the entire world system, unifying it into a one-world religion. Unity under the banner of love and growth is its platform promise, desirable now at all costs; this seems good, so the world accepts it (Genesis 3:6 says that Eve found the fruit good and desirable). But Revelation says "Mystery Babylon" is really the ancient enemy of God and, like the Babylon of old, it will present death as an angel of light, a dear friend, a fragrant visitation, a bliss realm of the music of the spheres, in perfect accord with the present Eastern mystical view of death. Only one major view challenges it, and Revelation proclaims that view also, with awesome power. Our aim must be to examine carefully the real implications of each side.

4

Finding a Definition for Death

Before going to the "other side," let us find an acceptable definition of death that we all can agree on. When is someone really dead? What is a standard on which medicine, law, science, and common sense can agree?

We certainly would be doubtful about reports of someone who "died" every afternoon at three o'clock, who snored through the experience, and revealed his tales of the other side as he rubbed the sleep out of his eyes. We would suspect he had been dreaming.

Yet what are we to say about the new hard-to-define nether worlds which are the recent products of medical technology? Was the patient dead whose electroencephalogram (EEG) floated for two hours? Opinion is divided. "Clinical death" is a more chimerical gray region than one might think.

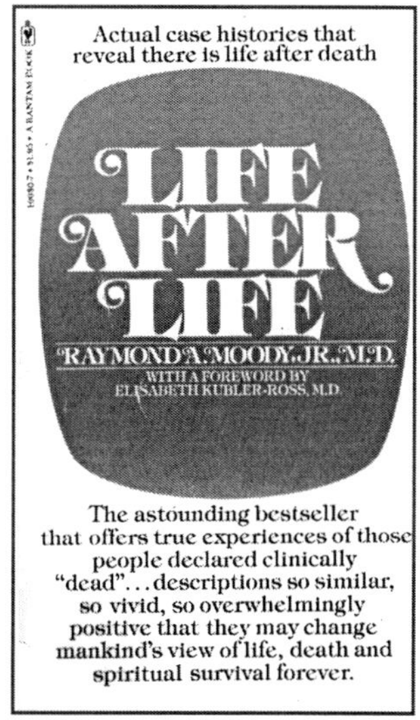

Actual case histories that
reveal there is life after death
LIFE
AFTER
LIFE
RAYMOND A. MOODY, JR., M.D.
WITH A FOREWORD BY
ELISABETH KUBLER-ROSS, M.D.
The astounding bestseller
that offers true experiences of those
people declared clinically
"dead"... descriptions so similar,
so vivid, so overwhelmingly
positive that they may change
mankind's view of life, death and
spiritual survival forever.

For the *Life After Life* study that Moody did, there were two general categories of subjects: those diagnosed as "clinically dead," and those who merely came close to death and reported their experiences. So the essence of Moody's report is among that minority of clinically dead out of the fifty subjects interviewed. We know that the latter group never died, but what about the first group?

For one thing, John Weldon, author of *Is There Life After Death?*, discovered at the outset of his investigation that a current problem exists among the authorities of even agreeing on a definition. Weldon observes, "Death had been defined recently in the courts as, 'Not a continuing event... [but] an event that takes place at a precise time.' Medical journals have it as, 'A process and not a moment in time."[1]

Weldon goes on to observe, "Considering those who were certified dead by machine—were they really dead, and how dead? There are still some problems here. Physicians, lawyers, and laymen ultimately disagree as to the moment or process of death."[2] And even physicians can disagree among themselves.

Are clinical-death patients who later revive perhaps an index not of death, but rather of the inadequacies of machine diagnosis? A machine seems to say for a while that a man is dead, but later it indicates life in the patient after all. Would a far more sensitive machine have registered "life" and not "death"?

A major current definition of death is "the absence of brain wave activity." This is a definition wholly dependent upon machine diagnosis. Is it 100 percent reliable?

"The EEG machine is a complicated one, difficult to set up, especially in emergency situations. Even practiced professionals are predisposed to confusion and error in the face of impending death. Getting correct readings is difficult. Secondly, there have been cases where flat EEG tracings (indicating no brain wave activity whatever) were obtained in people who were later resuscitated. This situation tends to occur in cases involving very low body temperatures .... Flat EEG readings in these cases (heart surgery etc.) have gone on for 24 hours in patients who then completely recovered."3

Then, too, disagreement exists among medical doctors as to how long the EEG reading should be flat before the patient is finally declared clinically dead. In hopes of preventing anyone from being murdered, "the National Academy of Medicine of France chose the 48-hour flat EEG reading for certifying death in the case of transplant donors."[4]

It appears from examining the results of our machine-diagnosed clinical death that we really do have a hit-or-miss situation. A subject is declared clinically dead before he has been found to be alive again after all. Did he die?

It becomes apparent that the clinical-death definition of death is inadequate, for it has loopholes. It is not good enough to satisfy the demands of science, because it contradicts the idea of an irreversible decision. (It got its definition in the past because people did not come back. Like the grave digger holding the skull, we knew so-and-so was dead.) But, in the past, medical practitioners found a very high correlation between "respiratory cessation," "cardiac arrest," complete "loss of vital signs," and the patients staying that way and not coming back.

Is there any other criterion besides clinical death? Yes, and it excludes every single one of Moody's subjects, as Moody himself anticipates. The most acceptable criterion for genuine and complete death occurs when the categories of "cardiac arrest," "respiratory cessation," "flat EEG," and "complete loss of vital signs" are satisfied and this condition remains permanent through rigor mortis and physical decay. When the body begins to smell from decay, one can be assured that it is dead, especially if it has been ice-cold for days and has gone through rigor mortis.

The only historical records of recoveries from this form of death are in the New Testament. Lazarus was stone cold and decaying for four days before he was brought back to live out the appointed remainder of his life. Death, apart from some really astounding miracle such as the case of Lazarus, is irreversible; that has to be the definition. If you protest this, then give us the death experience of a subject who has been dead four days and in decay, and we will be much more likely to be persuaded by the report.

But we are still left with a question. If Moody's subjects were never really dead, how do we explain their common pattern of experience? What is the origin or source of these experiences? As in any sound investigation, we will be pressed to look for other common patterns or precedents in history and ask, When, where, and in what context have the same experiences occurred before? Thanatologist Kubler-Ross strays from "science" occasionally and breathes a clue as to where to look; it is in the category of psychic mediums, psychics, yogis, and Eastern masters. "From my interviews with the dying and with MEDIUMS, I would describe the other world as similar to ours."[8] As we shall find out, her dealings in the "other traditions," the psychic occult, have been more than superficial. She herself has a spirit guide with whom she has been in contact for years. What we need to discover is whether there is a common ground linking yoga, Eastern beliefs, psychic teachings, and mediumistic contacts, especially if they converge so closely in their reports and proclamations about the nature of death. It may well turn out that all these groups stem from a common source; indeed, they could well be the new Babylonians.

Moody's clinically dead may be in a state that is far closer to a mediumistic trance or a yogic *samadhi* than real death. In *The Tibetan Book of the Dead*, a majority of the pre death reports on death came from yogis who had learned to enter a type of suspended animation. This still happens today. In October 1977, when I was in Delhi, a day-by-day, front-page news sensation concerned a yogi who was buried underground. He had managed to stop his heart for long periods, reduced his pulse rate to nil, lower his body temperature, and maintain a flat EEG. His gamble was that he could remain that way for ten days. The paper reported that when he had done the same thing in the 1960s, he was able to maintain the state for five days.' As we shall see later, yogis have traditionally sought this odd nether-world state; but because they came back and never showed the signs of absolute death, we know they never really died. Nor do they claim to have died.

If we were to try to figure out the mystery of existence, of life and death, we would have a limited number of options, which have been used in one way or another across history:

- We could ingest a consciousness altering substance such as ancient Soma or LSD and allow the experience to tell us the hidden secrets of life (Carlos Castaneda and Timothy Leary took this path).
- We could find mystics, mediums, gurus, shamans and yogis whose own experiences claim to solve our quest for ultimate truth. Castaneda and Leary also took this path. And it can include Hinduism, Kabbala, neopaganism, Sufism and other mystical paths.
- We could seek our own mystical revelation, some inner consciousness-expansion through some vision quest, yoga or mystical trance like so many of today's New Agers.
- We could attempt to use the instruments of science to somehow seek out the invisible parameters of life—the approach of ratio-

nalism, naturalism, and modernism.

■ We could attempt, as did Immanuel Kant, to apprehend the truth by sheer human reason. We would puzzle things out by using the logical and philosophical methods available, though we would probably end up like the rationalist philosophers limited to strictly observable phenomena which not even they, in the end, trusted. Also the approach of rationalism, naturalism, and modernism.

■ Finally, we could be left with one main option. If the order and complexity of the universe somehow testified of an Author, Creator, or God ... it might cross our minds that He Himself might well reach down (if life does have a purpose), and shortcut what might be a fruitless search by telling, directly, certain absolute truths of life and existence to a whole lineage of people—from ancient prophets to appointed saints. This is known as divine revelation; history, archeology, and good honest observation show that this possibility is by no means foreclosed. It makes a tremendous amount of sense when you think about it.

Actually, these six sub categories (apart from the nihilist, existentialist view, which believes everything is an accident), fall in either of the two major religious traditions: (1) the occult, Babylonian, Eastern, pantheistic-monistic tradition, with its preceptors ranging from mediums, psychics, yogis, avatars, and so on; or (2) the biblical tradition, with its prophets, saints, apostles, and one Christ.

Almost every book today which tackles the problem of the meaning of life tries to yoke the biblical and occult traditions and say that they both reveal the same truth and that both point to the same God. Since the life-after-death issue will inevitably lead us into one of these camps, we must examine whether they are compatible. Our conclusions about the two traditions will determine our attitudes toward death and will affect our behavior in life, so it is here we must begin.

5

Psychics Riding the Deathplane

On many freezing winter nights in 1968, I motorcycled down the dark wooded lanes weaving from Charlottesville, Virginia, to the spectral ranch house of Robert Monroe, author of *Journeys out of the Body*, poised on its many acres and beaming multicolored lights like an airport control tower. I was a student at the University of Virginia and in the throes of my own energized leap into the realms of mystical revelation, soon intending to head out to India to reach full enlightenment. Indeed, my friend Bob Monroe was famous across America among connoisseurs of the underground new-consciousness movement as a legitimate astral projector (one apparently able to leave the physical body). Charles Tart and an array

Tal Brooke and Robert Monroe

of notable parapsychologists had repeatedly run a whole gamut of double-blind tests on Monroe, invariably baffled each time by his unaccounted for powers. Monroe and I often met weekly.

Monroe and I originally met at a meeting of the Universal Youth Corps, which was founded by Dr. George Ritchie, a mystic and medical doctor to whom Dr. Moody dedicated his best seller, *Life After Life*, and who wrote the full account of his own death experience in *Return from Tomorrow*, Chosen Books, 1978. But by 1968 Ritchie had disbanded that group (though he remained in personal contact with some of us) because of some higher revelation.

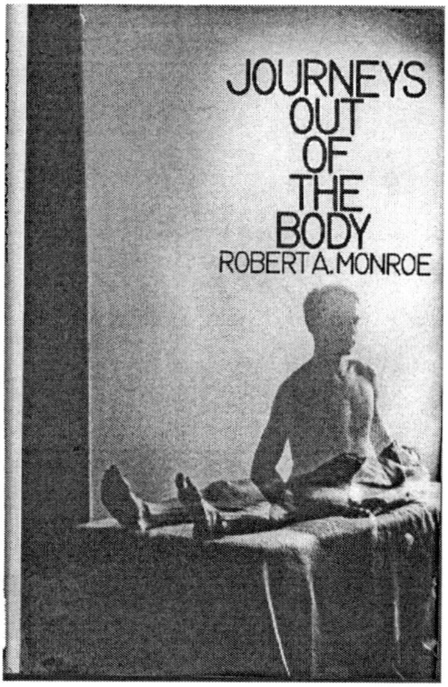

Monroe, a board member of Ritchie's Universal Youth Corps, was among the guest speakers to address the corps of mostly U.Va. students, along with Bryant Reeves, author of *Flying Saucer Pilgrimage* and a board member of Edgar Cayce's Association for Research and Enlightenment (A.R.E.). Monroe shared the enigmas of his many out-of-the-body travels—enigmas that later bound Monroe and me together in our own mutual quests following the dissolution of Ritchie's youth corps.

Monroe and I tried to make sense out of the whole phenomenon of astral travel, catalyzing one another in the process as we often met weekly. He was approaching the subject in terms of the "higher teachings" he had received while out of the body in his encounters with "higher beings, astral masters, and beings of light," combined with his diversified readings in yoga, Eastern thought, and scientific theory.

I was approaching his bizarre exploits and spirit encounters (plus a few of my own) from the viewpoint of non dualist Indian philosophy, through the perspective of my own 1966 mystical LSD experience—at which time I had experienced total unity of the universe—combined with a sort of mystical Christianity (along the lines of Ritchie, Cayce, Carl Jung, Paul Tillich, and Teilhard de Chardin).

To Monroe, perhaps my most important credential was that apparently I, too, had been able to leave my physical body. It had started when I was an eleven-year old child battling the mumps in London a year after getting the Ouija board.

Half asleep in bed, I would become paralyzed, hear the sound of jets, and apparently go ripping through the roof to hover above our house. Occasionally the same thing happened during my teens, and it was starting again in college. Monroe's out-of-the-body symptoms matched mine point for point.

During this era, I unwittingly found myself working with Monroe on the tape prototypes that eventually would become the M-5000 program, a complex, multi channel recorded tape which would be used across the country to induce astral experiences in the uninitiated. Cables and sound equipment trailed through the house from central command, an isolated geodesic chamber of pyramidal glass which rippled with colored lights, while pulse generators whirred and hummed to the syncopated beats of an organ. Monroe had been a child prodigy, spending much of his life dabbling with inventions (much of his experience coming from his New York era as vice-president of Mutual Broadcasting).

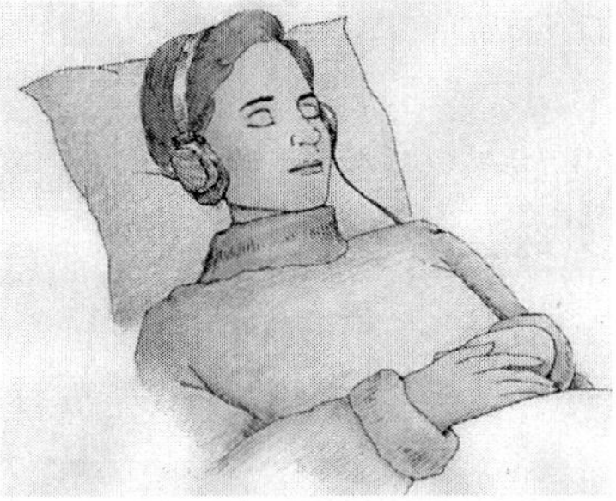

But what was most momentous was that we were on the pioneering frontier of **occult technology**! Indeed, it was from the "higher sources" that Monroe received the technological formulations of his endeavor (Monroe had a long list of technological breakthroughs that had been inspired by spirit contacts, the invention of the Xerox machine being a prime example). We were not closing the gap to enter the spiritual dimensions by blindly putting together the machinery. The powers on the other side had bridged the gap, with Monroe as medium, and were telling him exactly how to put things together. It is important that this be understood.

To be sure, our exploits had an air of intrigue. Imagine transforming America into a spiritual technology—another Atlantis—with at least half the population astral traveling one day! According to Monroe, Ritchie, Cayce, and others, such large-scale mass spirituality has not been seen since the "days of Atlantis."

But I still had problems with Monroe's "contact teachings" because they did not coincide with what I then considered the highest truth of all: the ultimate oneness of all things, which is the heart of Indian philosophy. To me, his "contact teachings" from astral classes given by "higher beings" were little more than fragmented interpretations of reality taught by demigods, beings of light, or spirits, which certainly were higher up than most humans, but still fell short of "the Absolute." As the Hindus would say, even that was a part of maya ("the illusory bondage of the ephemeral universe of appearances"). I tried to convince Monroe that the highest truth was the concept of the "static eternal" taught by Ramakrishna and the Indian mystics, for I was sure these sages had gone deeper than the meanderings of intermediate demigods. This fact alone eventually caused a split between Monroe and me. I went on to India, while he pursued his quest for the M-5000 and beyond.

Yet an aspect of some of our encounters threatened both our notions of a peril-free universe void of absolute evil (the "cosmic playground"

approach). Some of these spirit encounters had a brutal, almost demonic, concreteness. This cut away at the stereotype I was forming of an almost symphonically gentle and peace-pervading cosmos whose evil was so wispy and illusory that apparent evil was little other than beneficent playacting.

One Saturday morning in the spring of 1968, Monroe looked quite shaken as he rubbed his bleary eyes over a cup of coffee at our usual meeting place, the kitchen table. I had spent a fitful night alone in a far-wing bedroom, with earphones on while lying flat on my back in an attempt to enter what I called "the buzz region" for "lucid dreaming." Apparently Monroe had been assaulted by something at about three in the morning, and the encounter continued until dawn.

"I felt about as significant as an ant compared to these two beings," Monroe started off. He said he had perceived clairvoyantly two massive beings of light, brighter than stars and of vast power, drifting deep in the heavens like two meteors. Then they had stopped their drift and honed in on him, beginning a terrible drilling down upon him like huge, sparking hornets. They descended with great speed while Monroe remained in the paralyzed "buzz state." Reaching his room, they impersonally scanned the hidden records of his mind, flashing through his mind like flipping through a hard drive. After ten minutes they evidently had gotten what they wanted—or, as he suggested later, implanted what they wanted—and then pulled away, much like a huge hypodermic being pulled out of a patient. This experience brought up the question of victimization and cosmic bullying, but we preferred to theorize more in the direction that the incident was an act of charity, that the two beings probably had left a subtle implant which would germinate years later—perhaps as a clue to spiritual technology.

Robert Monroe

In a guarded manner, Monroe said that these two beings might have some connection with unidentified flying objects. He believed UFOs were not necessarily machines, but celestial beings, almost angels of a sort. Now and then, late at night, Monroe would drive on higher impulse to the area of Browns Mountain. Odd phenomena would occur, but he would not say much about it. Browns Mountain, in the Virginia Blue Ridge Mountains, was a notorious location for unusual occurrences, especially UFOs.

One common bond between Monroe and Ritchie was the UFO question and its role in what they saw as the *coming earth changes* (Researchers such as John Weldon, Ron Rhodes, and Bill Alnor agree that such strange UFO phenomena, which have been documented so many times, are really spiritual phenomena, both deceptive and demonic in nature.).

Revelation at Massanetta Springs

In the winter of 1972, a mere week after I returned to America following two years in India (a drama worthy of an 800 page manuscript eventually published as *Avatar or Night*), I was invited by my old friend Dr. George Ritchie to be a main speaker at a retreat in Massanetta Springs, Virginia. He also invited me to again join his Universal Youth Corps which he had started up again.

During this big retreat at Massanetta Springs, Ritchie disclosed something to an audience of two hundred people that finalized the tie between his mission and Bob Monroe's. (It was also something that soon created a barrier between Ritchie and myself, for by then I was a *former* mystic who had become a Christian.) Ritchie announced that in 1958, at another corps retreat at the Peaks of Otter, he had an experience one night that revealed his true mission on the earth. A voice (whom he called "God") told him to leave his tent and go out on the mountain. It then instructed him to observe the firmament of brilliant lights above, which he did. Next it told Ritchie that these lights were massive "mother ships, UFOs of five miles in diameter, numbering sixty thousand," and poised waiting for the celestial command to come swooping down to pick up the remnant of true believers on the earth before our planet plunged into darkness and catastrophe. Ritchie was informed that **he** was the new Noah of this age and that the vehicles used would be flying saucers. Like Abraham, Ritchie was promised that many would be in his fold.

My reaction was distress and amazement at not only the grandiosity of the vision—so typical of other self-proclaimed World Teachers who speak in grandiose language (as in Benjamin Creme as the John the Baptist of Maitreya)—but I knew now that Biblical exegesis clearly showed that God did not need to rely on the technology of spaceships to bring about His will.

I realized at the Ritchie's retreat that I was hearing another demonization of biblical apocalyptic language which ultimately denied Christ's second advent as well as God's sovereign power over history. Ritchie's vision of UFOs being the Noah's ark of some apocalypse fit perfectly into another arena that the Bible has predicted: counterfeit revelations and teachings that would increasingly deluge the world through false prophets and false Christs (Matt. 24:24) for the purpose of spiritual deception.

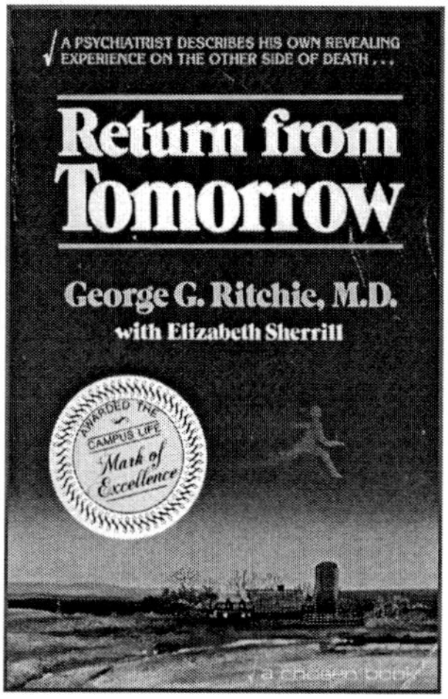

Monroe and Ritchie could both boast of *experience*, but what was the primary source of their individual inspirations? A being of light! Ritchie is the unspoken superstar of Moody's book. Ritchie's death experience, the grandest of all, occurred in Barkeley, Texas, in the mid 1940s. He says he encountered a "being of light brighter than ten billion arc welders," which proceeded to take him on a tour of the universe via different death planes and astral levels.

But behind it all is the cosmology of reincarnation and of man perfecting himself to become God, a being of light. *Karma* emerges, along with all the other pantheistic notions. Christ, Ritchie says, is a being of light. But that is not what the Bible says of the ascended Son of God, who is above "every name that is named" (Eph. 1:21).

There is one Christ, but many beings of light. Let us look into this network of beings and discern the intentions behind their variant theologies.

One predominant theme emerges: these beings of light and channeled entities have an obsessive preoccupation with Christ. Somehow they must deal with him before they can go on. Appearing to be loyal to biblical tradition, they obscure the simple heart of the gospel message. Naturally, they speak through people; their ideas come through human channels, mediums. Invariably, they also distort Christ so that he becomes a different Christ. As Paul the apostle warned in Galatians 1:6-9 (Phillips), we learn that this is an old problem:

> I am amazed that you have so quickly transferred your allegiance from Him Who called you in the grace of Christ to another "gospel"! Not, of course, that it is or ever could be another gospel, but there are obviously men who are upsetting your faith with a travesty of the Gospel of Christ. Yet I say that if I, or an angel from heaven, were to preach to you any other gospel than the one you have heard, may he be accursed! (Galatians 1:6-9)

It becomes apparent that "somebody" does not want biblical teaching to be accepted as it is without being filtered through another system, which is a most elaborate and costly strategy. As the old missionary saying goes, "Satan will use ninety-nine parts of the truth just to float one single lie." Yet most of these "Christs" that we shall examine barely contain one-tenth of the truth.

We already have seen that the beings of light reviewed by Moody disavow biblical judgment. Christ becomes a being of light, reincarnation is offered as a viable option, and God is almost avoided entirely. Is there a common pattern among the most famous mediums?

6

Breakthroughs of the Spirit World

Our battle is to bring down every deceptive fantasy and every imposing defense that men erect against the true knowledge of God (2 Cor. 10:5, 6, Phillips).

Edgar Cayce, the clear-eyed, bespecled Kentuckian who looked as honest as the day is long is without a doubt the greatest channeler of the 20th century, producing a library of metaphysical teachings from his decades of psychic readings and mediumistic trances.

A veritable Bible-Belt medium, Cayce originally won many hearts by his heartening, almost sentimental, allegiances to Christ, and the reverential tones in which he couched his deviant teaching. This man of such plain and humble demeanor seemed to be far from any calculating card shark.

Yet if we look in Proverbs, we find that

there is more to judge than honest looks. A man can appear good and yet deceive. Second Corinthians 11:15 says Satan's ministers appear "as ministers of righteousness."

Cayce helped me go to India. The "Christ" he was weaving fit perfectly into what I had learned from George Ritchie as well as the philosophies of the East. This was a major bridge for me. The dialogue of Cayce's trance readings would go from an impersonal "we" of the so-called cosmic mind ("*Akashic records*") to a pseudo King James Bible talk of "ye" and "thee." What emerged from his filtering system was a most complex schema. Boiled down, it amounted to this: Christ was the perfect yogi, avatar, ("incarnation"), and God-man, who had reincarnated on the earth a number of times in setting up his messianic mission, perfecting himself with each life. Melchizedek was but one embodiment in Christ's genealogy of past lives. In that sense he becomes a model for all men to follow in order to attain what is now called "Christ-consciousness," a level of cosmic awareness at the pinnacle of soul evolution.

Along with rebirth comes the inevitable law of karma. Sin disappears and the biblical God vanishes into something that is more like Brahman. As Cayce gave people "life readings" concerning their past lives, they were told they were ex-high priests from Atlantis, ex-wizards, psychic healers, and occasionally a former disciple of Christ, doubtlessly returned to touch up here and there the blemishes of the past.

One biographer compiled a book just about Cayce's teachings on Christ by sifting through thousands of "life readings" filed at the A.R.E. at Virginia Beach. What emerges, of course, is an emphasis on the *hidden years* of

Christ's life, about which the Bible is silent.

With an elaborate discourse on astrological forces, we see the young "perfect Master" headed to Egypt to study at the temples of wisdom and beauty, where he learns certain psychic arts. Then He goes on to India and Tibet to learn levitation and transmutation from certain Tibetan masters; while in India, he learns healing, weather control, telepathy, and ultimately reaches atonement ("at-one-ment") with the divine overmind. From there he returns to the Holy Land as the fully promised Messiah.

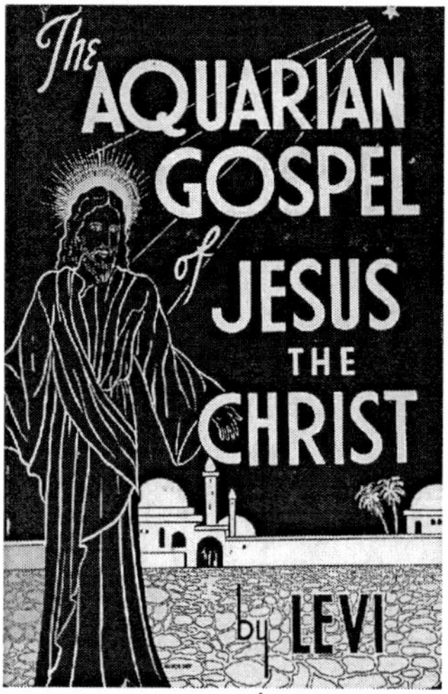

Yet the apostles left out all this information. The Bible does not mention so much as a hint of it, and none of the historians of antiquity even had the slightest notion of any of this.

Practically all of the psychics, mediums, and mystics portray this brand of cosmic Christ. Levi Dowling fares no better. His book, *The Aquarian Gospel of Jesus the Christ*, was written in the later nineteenth century, while this Midwestern psychic and medical practitioner traveled from town to town in a covered wagon. This particular gospel, currently most popular and fashionable, was written through the medium from midnight to three in the morning as he gave his body over to a "higher force" to write through him. Its purpose? It completes what the apostles left out, updated for our present "Aquarian age," which is interesting considering the Bible's stand against the Babylonian occult science of astrology. Dowling, like the other mediums, started out early by a deliberate rejection of the Christian message.

Thomas Sugrue, the major biographer of Edgar Cayce in *There Is a River*, makes an observation that fits both Cayce and Dowling:

> The system of metaphysical thought which emerges from the readings of Edgar Cayce is a Christianized version of the mystery religions of ancient Egypt, Chaldea, Persia, India, and Greece. It fits the figure of Christ into the tradition of one God for all people, and places Him in His proper place... He is the capstone of the pyramid.

This is far removed from the true biblical Christ, who is the chief cornerstone of the living Church.

Dowling portrays the "young Master" as a sort of Siddhartha, passing tortuous tests, transcending the limited ego, and going on sojourns through India, Tibet, Persia, Assyria, Greece, and Egypt.

To establish this point clearly, we will examine a number of statements from this higher gospel, the so-called Aquarian gospel. Of course, we see an entirely different story, teaching, and personality than what appears in the New Testament. Both cannot be right.

> And Jesus was accepted as a pupil in the temple Jagannath: and here learned the Vedas and Manic laws (21:19).
>
> Benares of the Ganges was a city rich in culture and learning; here the two rabbonis tarried many days. And Jesus sought to learn the Hindu art of healing, and became the pupil of Udraka, the greatest of Hindu healers. Udraka taught the uses of the waters, plants, and earths; of heat and cold; sunshine and shade; of light and dark (23:2-4). [This is herbalist arts.]
>
> [Jesus teaches at the house of Udraka.] And Jesus said to them, With much delight I speak to you concerning life—the brotherhood of life. The universal God is one, yet he is more than one; all things are God; all things are One (28:3, 4). [This is pantheism, monism.]
>
> [Jesus hears of the grief of his mother over the death of Joseph, his "father." He assures her that Joseph's round of karma is completed.] Why should you weep? Tears cannot conquer grief. There is no power in grief to mend a broken heart. The Plane of grief is idleness; the busy soul can never grieve; it has no time for grief (30:11, 12). [This is a contradiction to his tears and indignation of spirit at the tomb of Lazarus.]
>
> [Jesus attends a feast in Persepolis and speaks to the people, reviewing the magician philosophy.] A feast in honor of the magician God was being held, and many men were gathered in Persepolis. And on the great day of the feast the ruling magician master said, Within these sacred walls is liberty; whoever wills to speak may speak. And Jesus standing in the midst of the people, said, My brothers, sisters, children of our Father-God; most blessed are you among the sons of men today, because you have just conceptions of the Holy One and man. Your purity in worship and in life is pleasing unto God; and to your master Zarathustra, praise is due. [He later explains to the magicians that their human will must merge into divine will.] [39:1-5). [This is occultic and syncretistic.]
>
> [Jesus runs into the Oracle at Delphi.] Apollo said to Jesus, Sir, if you would see the Delphic Oracle, and hear it speak, you may accompany me .... And when Apollo stood before the Oracle it spoke and said:

> Apollo, sage of Greece, the bell strikes twelve; the midnight of the ages has come .... The Delphic age has been an age of glory and renown; the gods have spoken to the sons of men through oracles of wood, and gold, and precious stone. •.. The gods will speak to man by man. The living oracle now stands within these sacred groves; the Logos from on High has come (45:3-10). [Idolatry is justified; Christ becomes the oracle through which the gods are to speak.]

> [In Heliopolis of Egypt, Jesus goes through the seven tests of the mystical brotherhood. Test number six is in the Chamber of the Dead.] The senior course of study now was opened up and Jesus entered and became a pupil of the Heirophant. He learned the secrets of the mystic lore of Egypt land; the mysteries of life and death and of the worlds beyond the circle of the Sun. When he had finished all the studies of the senior course, he went into the Chamber of the Dead, that he might learn the ancient methods of preserving from decay the bodies of the Dead; and here he wrought. And the carriers brought the body of a widow's only son to be embalmed; the weeping mother followed close; her grief was great. And Jesus said, Good Woman, dry your tears; you follow an empty house; your son is in it not. You weep because your son is dead. Death is a cruel word; your son can never die (54:1-71. [This contradicts the Genesis curse and advocates astrology; Christ raised the dead, not embalmed them; it advocates the Egyptian mysteries, etc.]

Levi Dowling's book and Edgar Cayce's teachings reveal a "Christos" of the mystery religions and mystical orders—a false Christ who has become a kind of deceptive cornerstone of New Age spirituality.

And in the decaying edifices of Christendom, made barren by the endless sorties of the scholarship of doubt, propelled by liberal and modernist hermeneutics so exemplified by the Jesus Seminar, what is to keep church leaders from seeking after mediums? Nothing. After all, the church as been made empty. And the exploits of Bishop James Pike has now been embraced by large segments of the mainline denominations by the end of the 20th century.

Bishop James Pike

Arthur Ford, a Canadian billed constantly as "the greatest medium of the century," was the man who "turned on" Bishop James Pike. His Christ fits quite handily into the mold dictated by the so-called Spiritualist Church. Ford, who boasted, "I've slept for the best people," did a noteworthy job on Bishop Pike in adding to the delusion of the already apostate bishop.[2]

Indeed, what really launched spiritualism in post-60s America was the Bishop Pike incident. Pike once told theologian Francis Schaeffer that all he was left with after coming out of a liberal Union seminary was "a hand full of stones." After meeting Ford, however, Pike lost not only that, but more: his life.

Proudly jettisoning plain biblical teaching, Bishop Pike was now ripe for a "higher" breakthrough. It came in the form of a spirit masquerading as Jim, his dead son. His own crippled faith could not deal with Jim's death, so he turned to his disembodied son for the answer. Pike invited the public to watch a televised seance of himself and Arthur Ford. This potent propaganda presented the perfect opportunity for the spirits to teach the public about higher truth.

The so-called spirit of Jim originally started the contact by extensive poltergeist phenomena in the bishop's apartment—heat changes, levitating objects, disappearing objects, and, at one point, chopping off the bangs of a woman visitor, Maren Bergrud.

Pike went to Ena Twigg, an English medium, and found out that the spirit was "Jim." Jim told the bishop, "Since I've been here, I haven't heard anything about Jesus." Some months later at another seance, Jim added, "This was religion without somebody forcing God and Jesus down my throat .... I haven't met [Jesus]. They talk about him—a mystic, a seer, yes, a seer. Oh, but Dad, they don't talk about him as a savior. As an example, you see?... Don't you ever believe that God can be personalized. He is the Central Force and you give your quota toward it. Do you agree with me, Dad?"[3] The bishop responded like a good dad should and jumped in with both feet, carrying a few million bystanders with him.

Channeler Arthur Ford played the largest role in unhinging Pike's theology and setting him up for the kill, ultimately directing the bishop and his new wife out to the Judean Desert. There they became stranded and the bishop wandered off into heat-filled mirages to die, while his young wife went off looking for help. Since then, the Ouija boards have been clacking away, heedless of biblical injunctions, to pick up the latest gleanings of higher truth from the now-departed bishop.

Now another pattern appears. Those mediums who did not start out by directly dabbling in the occult got their first boost by some kind of trauma. Allen Spraggett calls this a well-attested fact in his book, *Arthur Ford: The Man Who Talked with the Dead.* He adds, "Edgar Cayce, as a child, was knocked unconscious by a baseball and thereafter gave evidence of his remarkable powers. The contemporary Dutch-born clairvoyant, Peter

Hurkos, fell off a ladder when he was twenty—lobotomizing himself—and woke up a mind reader."[4] Similar examples are cited by Spraggett regarding Ronald Ewin, D.D. Home, Clement Stone, and Arthur Ford.

Almost all of these mediums were exposed directly to Eastern mysticism—Cayce through a theosophist in Chicago, and Arthur Ford by delving into theosophy. Then in 1920 Ford met Yogananda, joined one of his yoga classes, started meditating, and "maintained years later" that it was "Yogananda who taught him how to induce a yogic trance, and, equally important, how to manipulate that altered state of consciousness for mediumistic purposes."5 That is how Ford learned astral projection.

Therefore, it is not surprising that Ford, like the rest, also pushed the concepts of reincarnation, karma, and an impersonal pantheistic God.[6]

Spraggett, his biographer, sums it up: "For Arthur Ford, then, as for many spiritualists, Jesus Christ was a mirror of God; but he was not a quasi-divine savior whose death on the cross redeems man from sin."

"Spiritualists," Ford is quoted as saying in a 1930 sermon, "can't depend on Christ. We must stand on our own feet. The spiritualist is the supreme individualist. We will eradicate our own sins, even though it takes a whole eternity in which to work them out!"

"Spiritualism," Spraggett observes, "like Buddhism, declares that man is his own savior, that the only salvation is self-salvation, that being saved by proxy is as impossible as learning by proxy, for, in both Buddhism and spiritualism, the key to salvation is right knowledge."

Ford's biographer then shares a most apropos declaration: "When we come to consider the distinctive teachings of Spiritualism, namely, its view of the afterlife and of communication between this world and the next, we find that it diverges even more markedly from traditional Christian thought."[7]

In line with most spiritualists, Kubler-Ross shared her own impressions of the afterlife when she said, "From my interviews with the dying and with mediums, I would describe the other world as looking similar to ours, except for the colors, which are very vibrant."[8]

Last but not least in the lives of mediums are their manner of life and the ends they come to. By the standard of Christ's teaching that you should know a man by his fruit (in the fullest sense of character and actions), mediums bear a rather wrinkled and sour fruit.

Ford was a miserable example of his own proud declaration, "We must stand on our own feet." Spraggett takes us through Ford's tortured personal life, his dope addiction, and then years of bouts with alcoholism, putting on a front before the public while pulling off mediumistic contacts, and then going back to long binges on the bottle. The famous medium died a wreck. His last words were, "God help me."[9]

The founders of modern spiritualism, Margaret and Kate Fox, who established spirit contact on March 21, 1848, and rose to prominence, also became alcoholics. They said the spirits had promised them protection, but it never came. "Craving for alcohol, they lost all sense of moral responsibility. Margaret, in the presence of her sister Kate at an anti-spiritualist meeting in 1888 declared, 'I am here tonight, as one of the founders of Spiritualism, to denounce it as absolute falsehood... the most wicked blasphemy the world has ever known.' [10] As they died, both mediums cursed God.

Spraggett documents a long list of mediums who lived lives of turmoil and pain. "Besides alcoholism and drug addiction, sexual excesses or aberrations seem to be common among mediums .... Mediumship takes a toll in human suffering. Henry Slade, the famed nineteenth-century slate-writing medium, died penniless and alcoholic in a Michigan sanatorium. Stainton Moses, a scholarly medium who was an Anglican priest, disintegrated into abject alcoholism. Veiled eroticism lurked in the seance room of Eusapio Palladino .... Many male mediums have been homosexual, or ambisexual. Some psychical researchers go so far as to suggest that a certain sexual ambiguity is a part of the mediumistic temperament."[11]

I personally heard from a number of sources closely connected with the A.R.E. that, during his last two weeks of life, Edgar Cayce was in abject fear that his source of revelation was not the "Akashic Mind" but, instead, some kind of baleful spirit power. Medium Cayce died a Christless death without peace.

Raphael Gasson

But one other witness, an exception, remains to be reviewed in our case. As a medium in London, he had contacted numerous spirits and beings of light, yet escaped the disastrous fate which befalls most mediums. How was Raphael Gasson spared? He became convinced that the source of his contacts was not the spirits of the departed, or higher beings of light, but, in fact, what he called "impersonating demons."

Gasson turned his life over to Jesus Christ, coming as a penitent sinner, without hope apart from Christ, and asking Christ to be his Lord and Savior. He suddenly realized that by the astoundingly holy standards of the living God, any effort on his part alone was futile. In contrast to Ford's proud declaration, Gasson *did* cry out for help, the sanest thing he could ever do. He was saved. Gasson claims that he was freed for the first time in his life, knew that he had a genuine reason for hope, and suddenly started changing as a person. In his book *The Challenging Counterfeit*, Gasson gives an inside look into the secrets of mediumship.

7 Principles of the Spiritualists National Union

For one thing, he reveals that the seven principles of the Spiritualists National Union, founded in 1891, almost matched Moody's conclusions perfectly. Keep in mind that the major goal of spiritualism is to prove life after death precisely in the manner Moody has. The principles are:

1. The Fatherhood of God.
2. The Brotherhood of Man.
3. The communion of saints and the ministry of angels.
4. Human survival after physical death.
5. Personal responsibility to answer for one's own sins.
6. Compensation or retribution for good or evil deeds.
7. Eternal progress of every soul."[12]

The most amazing thing to me about Gasson's book is the last third, where he delves into the intricate dynamics of mediumship, matching much of what I had gleaned after years of studying and practicing yoga in India. Gasson discusses astral projection, vacating the mind, vacating the body, blanking out of consciousness, how the other personality takes over, and the eventual acquisition of the powers of telepathy, clairvoyance, materialization of spirit presences (in the manner of the visitation Kubler-Ross spoke of), levitation, healing, the seeing of auras, the apports of physical objects, supernatural knowing, and so on.

Gasson, like all the other mediums, believed in reincarnation. The soul, they say, evolves after so many countless lifetimes. Spiritualists use the concept of reincarnation to explain away misfortune in life. For example, the spiritualistic explanation of a stillborn infant is "a spirit who has evolved over and over again and all that is needed to attain perfection was just one more very short period in a physical body after which it becomes a spirit of the highest evolution straight away. This belief extends to animals and insects who are gradually evolving until they become human beings, and so on."[13] In India today, one commonly hears similar explanations. A child bitten by a snake is just working off karma ("the total record of his past: good vs. bad deeds"), and his next body will be much higher up. If an Indian infant dies, it is often explained as a very high sage or yogi coming just to work off a smidgen of remaining bad karma. Then the yogi will reach "one with the absolute." (We begin to see that in more places than one the psychics, mediums, and spiritists are far closer in their beliefs to Hinduism than to biblical Christianity.) But what exactly is a "spirit of the highest evolution possible" to which Gasson refers?

Gasson reveals something that is crucial to our understanding of this whole matter: "Having attained the highest evolution in the spirit world, one becomes A BALL OF LIGHT."[14] Where have we seen this before? The highest stage of spiritual evolution is the "ball of light" or, as other spiritualist camps refer to it, "a being of light." Here is a vital clue to understanding the significance of Moody's beings of light.

In many of the original reports, Moody's subjects referred to the being of light as a "ball of light." They testified that the reason for life, as they had learned in the spirit world, was for the soul's growth or evolution. It only takes a second to make the connection: the ultimate of spiritual growth is a state of existence whereby one becomes a being of light, which is a major tenet of spiritualism. The view of afterlife in Moody's best seller, *Life After Life*, is in full accord with the teachings of mediums, psychics, and spiritualists. This doctrine, formally propounded by a worldwide organization known as the Spiritualists or the Spiritualist Church, is aligned with another view known as "spiritism." Both doctrines are antithetical to biblical doctrines, as we shall see.

What can be known about the actual spirit world? Where do the dead go? After abundant research, it becomes clear that the picture changes from medium to medium. Kubler-Ross says tamely that the spirit world is like ours, only the colors are brighter. Pike's son, Jim, says it is not as good as he hoped, that it is sort of murky, but that he hopes to figure it out more one day. Psychics and mediums like Cayce, Ritchie, and Ford speak of varying levels of death planes; their views are the closest to the accounts in *The Tibetan Book of the Dead.* Ritchie's report of his "Barkeley, Texas, experience" goes from hell worlds of imprisoned spirits (presumably killers and all brands of scum) to the dismal realms of "earth-bound souls," where the spirits of departed alcoholics try to jump into the bodies of living alcoholics. We then see mediocre spirit planes, much like our world, on up to the plane which Ritchie describes as "a city of light," where there are "beings of light." Long before Moody wrote *Life After Life*, he heard Ritchie give his account of the city of light and the beings of light. Ritchie says, and Moody intimates, that the ultimate destiny of the highest soul is to become a being of light and to live in the city of light. Many beings of light exist, including Christ, Buddha, and myriad others in their ranks.

Depiction of the Akashic Hall of Records on the deathplane

But our search into the world of mediums and psychics does not end here. We must look even further to do justice to our inquiry. We need to see more clearly whether there is blatant evidence to help us determine whether the forces surging through the mediums, in genuine cases, are neutral, good, or evil.

We need to ask the mediums—assuming the channeling is legitimate in the first place—"How do you know you can trust a voice of a being you have never seen? And if you tell me you know it is good, why should I trust you?"

8

Beings of Light or False Angels of Light?

"Dr. Elizabeth Kubler--Ross, whose work has revolutionized attitudes about death and dying, says the spirit of a deceased former patient helped dissuade her nine years ago from abandoning her work ... she since has become convinced that it was a 'spontaneous materialization of somebody who had died almost a year before.' Kubler Ross discussed the mysterious incident reluctantly. She said her experience' will sound so crazy that I wouldn't be surprised if people think, "Oh, she's now becoming an occultist, a spiritualist.""'

The incident occurred in her office at the University of Chicago, where she was an associate professor of psychiatry. She had organized a series of seminars on death and dying, in which terminally ill patients discussed their innermost feelings about facing death.

A woman appeared at her office and introduced herself as a patient who had died ten months before, Kubler-Ross says. The visitor looked identical to the former patient, but Kubler-Ross refused to believe it could be the same person.

"She said she knew I was considering giving up my work with dying patients and that she came to tell me not to give it up," Kubler-Ross recalls. "She said the time was not right. I reached out to touch her. I was reality testing. I was a scientist, a psychiatrist, and I didn't believe in such things.

"I told her a white lie and said I wanted her to write a little note I could give to her minister. The minister and I had helped this woman a lot. This way, you know, I thought I could check her out by the handwriting.

"She smiled in this all-knowing way, like she knew very well what my intentions were." But the woman wrote the note and signed it, and handwriting analysis indicated that it matched the handwriting of the deceased patient.

Kubler-Ross says the incident" came at a crossroads where I would have made the wrong decision if I hadn't listened to her," and that her subsequent work has convinced her "there is life after death." Pearre then proceeds to quote Kubler-Ross's involvement with mediumism as a source of evidence of afterlife. She has even worked out a system so that her deceased patients can get in touch with her. That short visit has resounded around the world, almost starting a crusade for death and dying. As already has been pointed out, the real Pandora's box that has opened has been the emergence of occult doctrine on a greater scale than before.

Since that time, Kubler-Ross has gotten to know her spirit guide, Salem, well enough for him to materialize in her room. For those who understand spiritism, that signifies a very advanced involvement. Exactly what she has learned from Salem in the way of advanced teachings, I cannot say, but I have a good idea. Whereas she has not revealed publicly what Salem has shared with her (though he could be preparing her to do so), the teachings of other spirit guides, or beings of light, are available. A profound connection exists among every one of these "higher teachings," which is far from accidental; indeed, it is most intentional, most timely, for history's present course.

In order to be heard as a scientific voice, Moody has to keep a cautious neutral distance from too much dogma. The scientific presentation requires an air of detachment, but be assured that some of the most effective editorializing comes from who is selected to say what. Moody, a partner and friend of Kubler-Ross's, appears to be more the scientist. It is important to review a few of his discoveries before proceeding. We will see the beginnings of "higher teachings," which have paved the way for more advanced teachings. Again, when the public climate is right, there is every possibility that the spirit guide of Kubler-Ross will use her as a mouthpiece.

Reviewing the Moody material briefly, the following subject is a man who saw a small "ball of light" hovering in an upper corner of his hospital room. The patient is then quoted by Moody:

I turned over and tried to get in a more comfortable position, but just at that moment a light appeared in the corner of the room, just below the ceiling. It was just a ball of light, almost like a globe, and it was not very large, I would say no more than twelve to fifteen inches in diameter, and as this light appeared, a feeling came over me. I can't say it was an eerie feeling, because it was not. •.. I could see a hand reach down for me from the light, and the light said, "Come with me. I want to show you something." So immediately, without any hesitation whatsoever, I reached up with my hand and grabbed onto the hand I saw. As I did, I had the feeling of being drawn up and of leaving my body, and I looked back and saw it lying there on the bed while I was going up towards the ceiling of the room.

... I took on the same form as the light. I got the feeling, and I'll have to use my own words for it,... that this form was definitely a spirit. It wasn't a body, just a wisp of smoke or a vapor. It looked almost like the clouds of cigarette smoke you can see when they are illuminated as they drift around a lamp. The form I took had colors, though ....

So, I was drawn up to the same position the light was in, and we started moving through the ceiling and the wall of the hospital room, into the corridor, and through the corridor, down through the floors it seemed, on down to a lower floor in the hospital.[2]

The patient and his spirit guide, as Moody relates in five pages of direct quotation, glide around and dialogue, the subject experiences feelings of great inner calm, and finally—like the classical magical wish—the being of light grants the patient a longer life. At the very least, this is an out-of-the-body experience combined with a spirit contact.

This episode is mediumistic by definition; it is as simple as that. The ensuing debate regarding the subject's willingness to participate in the experience, as opposed to his being a victim of something, is lengthy and complex. He himself says that without hesitation he extended his hand to the being. I am certain that he could have, or someone else would have, refrained. In some occult testimonies, people have prayed in fear and the presence left. Such has been true in my own life.

Moody tells of another interesting discovery: "In a few instances, people have come to believe that the beings they encountered were their 'guardian spirits. 'One man was told by such a spirit that, 'I have helped you through this stage of your existence, but now I am going to turn you over to others.' A woman told me that as she was leaving her body she detected the presence of two other spiritual beings there, and that they identified themselves as her 'spiritual helpers.'" 3 Then Moody reports that a number of people have come out of these experiences with psychic abilities.[4]

One of Moody's subjects says, "You know in your heart there's no such thing as death. You just graduate from one thing to another—like from grammar school to high school, to college." Another testimony follows: "Life is like imprisonment. In this state, we just can't understand what prisons these bodies are. Death is such a release—like an escape from prison. That's the best thing I can think of to compare it to." [5]

In the next few paragraphs, Moody completes what the Bible missed; he corrects it where it errs. But invariably he reminds us of the standard biblical caricatures, so that they will stay in our minds as representations of Christianity, and then he indulges in two sweeping statements that seem to demolish the paper dummies he has erected. "No one has described the cartoonist's heaven of pearly gates, golden streets, and winged, harp-playing angels, nor a hell of flames and demons with pitchforks." [6] In place of this caricature, which has nothing to do with true biblical revelation, comes an erudite and fair-minded improvement. Moody goes on: "So in most cases, the reward-punishment model of the afterlife is abandoned and disavowed, even by many who had been accustomed to thinking in those terms. They found, much to their amazement, that even when their most apparently awful and sinful deeds were made manifest before the being of light, the being responded not with anger and rage, but rather only with understanding, and even with humor."[7]

The one thing that the perfect God of the Bible does not find amusing is human sin as it manifests itself across a great spectrum of cruelties, dehumanizations, perversities, and rank horrors. The living God of Scripture will not greet Himmler, Goebbels, or Hitler with cosmic giggles of amused understanding. That would be a miscarriage of justice to the mangled victims and would not be good. Such cosmic tolerance, the contented good-neighbor policy with evil, ultimately spells a topsy-turvy universe whose "god" is insane or evil. True goodness, as a quality of deity, must be absolute.

What higher or more sublime good replaces the biblical caricatures? "In place of this old model, many seemed to have returned with a new model and a new understanding of the world beyond—a vision which features not unilateral judgement but rather cooperative development [and here Moody lets the cat out of the bag] towards the *ultimate* end of *Self-realization.*"[8]

That is Eastern mysticism, with the identical "self-realization" propounded in *The Tibetan* Book *of the Dead.* It is the final reward given those who have maneuvered through the obstacle course of bardos ("death planes"), those who have come to know "their essential nature," those whose eyes have remained on the pellucid "clear light." That "self-realization" is *moksha;* it is *Nirvana* ("enlightenment"). It appears that Moody uses the term *self-realization* most deliberately, for he *has* cited *The Tibetan Book of the Dead*, where this term is crucial to its view of the cosmos, and it is consistent with reincarnationist views. It appears to be no accident that Moody mentions Dr. Ian Stevenson's *Twenty* Cases Sugges*tive of Reincarnation* as further resource material (the same lan Stevenson who tried to arrange seances with the "greatest medium of the century," Arthur Ford, and who has been in contact with the most famous medium in America today, Jane Roberts, through whom "Seth" speaks). When you annihilate Christianity, there is only one great religious alternative; it is pantheism, it is Hinduistic mysticism. That is what Moody is leaving us with, and that is invariably the emergent "gospel" of his subjects who have become spirit contacts. This pattern is almost infallibly consonant with every contact that a subject or medium has had with a spirit, which I have ever studied. Christian doctrines are either tampered with or annihilated.

Jane Roberts—the First Wave of Channelers

Moody has opened the door. Although he has not given us the most significant information yet, he has told us a few key premises that lead to a definite place. We know that there is a higher plane of spirit, that there are spirits, that there are beings of light, that the whole scheme seems to be the evolution of the soul or self, and that many of these fascinating truths have come through people who have talked to beings of light or spirit guides.

Knowing all of this, if you and I should go on an excursion into the neighborhood drugstore or supermarket, we would be able to find on the average book rack numerous "higher revelations," which have come through a recent host of spirit contacts. If we are persuaded that these beings of light are out there for our own good and that they are our cosmic allies—and if we have become convinced of them through reading Moody—it will behoove us to listen attentively to what they are saying.

One of these books, a major occult best seller, flooded the book racks three years ago, and it and several other books by the same author are still best sellers. Like an old enemy on a street corner, it drew my eyes in recognition as, well past midnight, I stared at the gnarled face of Jane Roberts emerging from a purple paperback cover, contorting like a vampire in a Polish horror film. She had been photographed while" Seth" was taking over her body. I squinted my eyes in thought and looked off. Recalling my era in Egyptology, I said to myself, "Seth is the name of the Egyptian god of evil." Sure enough, when I checked it out in Webster's dictionary, it said: "Seth, n. an Egyptian god represented as having the head of a beast and a pointed snout. He was the brother of Osiris and the personification of physical evil and darkness, the adversary of good."

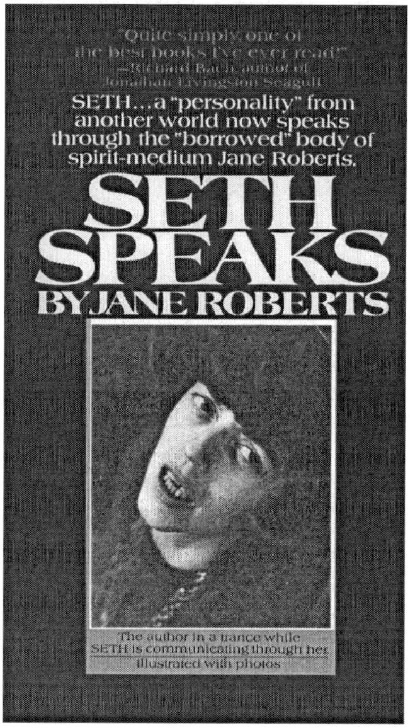

With irony, I remarked to myself under my breath, "And this is what the modern age has sought after to replace God: the infallible pride of science and humanism, the smugness, the mockers who sneer at the clear sanity of biblical revelation and then go groping after something that is such a travesty that it makes consummate fools of them all."

The Apostle Paul, in the Epistle to the Romans, states the ironic justice that pursues the willfully blind: "For even though they knew God, they did not honor Him as God, or give thanks; but they became futile in their speculations, and their foolish heart was darkened. Professing to be wise, they became fools, and exchanged the glory of the incorruptible God for an image" (Rom. 1:21-23, NASB).

The face of the medium on the cover was a dead giveaway. A normal child would sense it, and recoil in horror; yet here was a best-selling book about a modern medium and the creature that used her body as a mouthpiece to the world. The book by Jane Roberts is entitled *Seth Speaks*? Other books by Roberts would follow.

Jane Roberts, now deceased, has remained among the most prolific of all contemporary channelers. Her books have sold abundantly since the mid-70's. Rather than the usual fluffy afterlife affirmations, not only are her revelations more demanding and complex, they occasionally become quite unsettling, indeed, more blatantly evil.

It is an object lesson that what gets through is not always like a cheery cartoon character, but a dark and resourceful intelligence that is after something. Her experience contains, in dramatic form, all of the earmarks of a genuine medium being reached and controlled from the other side. It is a very compelling tale and throws light on more recent, attention seeking channelers such as J.Z. Knight, who channels Ramtha, or Van Praagh, for that matter, who is the latest sensation. In today's sanitized spotlight, you rarely see the twitches in the dark, the groans, the strange faces that tell you that maybe something abnormal is going on here—something that men were not made for. Perhaps there is a monster hiding in the darkness, and the reality is closer to an ancient vampire tale than the sanitized New Age explanations.

Jane Roberts became the channel for an entity named Seth. It started on an early September day in 1963. In her apartment in Elmira, New York, this aspiring novelist suddenly began to have some very strange experiences. Her encounters changed her life as well as the lives of thousands of people who have since read her numerous bestsellers that fill the New Age/Occult sections of countless bookstores.

This is the drama that took place in the life of the modern medium, as recorded in The Seth Material by Roberts: The scenario is a liberated literary graduate of Skidmore University portrayed as an honest seeker of truth who convinces us that her ventures into the occult were innocent, natural, and in no way premeditated. She just happened to stumble over a Ouija board one day as her husband, out of the blue, recommended that she write a book on ESP. On the night of December 8, 1963, the Ouija board's pointer began to move. That was when the doorway opened and Seth entered their lives. The first messages were sufficiently profound, endearing, and casual to pull them in. The spirit was called "Frank Withers," of all innocuous names; a local dead man, so to speak. But soon it said that it preferred not to be called Frank Withers. When they asked what to call it, the reply was, "To God, all names are his name." Then it said, "You may call me whatever you choose. I call myself Seth, it fits the me of me."

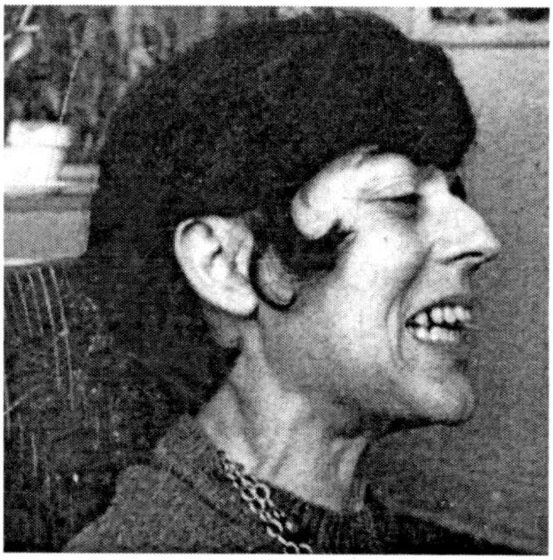

Channeling Seth

After several sessions, Jane, the medium, began to anticipate the words in her mind before the pointer spelled them out on the Ouija board. In her description of the transition she says that the pointer paused, and she felt as if she were standing at the top of a high diving board. It was as if she were trying to make herself jump while people were waiting impatiently behind her. She took the leap, and for the first time she began to speak for Seth. The words continued the sentences the board had spelled out. The being acted like a jocular, wise, paternal old friend from some past life. Yet it made no mistake in showing that it was fully superhuman and, among other things, trying to get across to this world the wisdom that it was only now ready for.

With the innocent tone of a high school girl following a cooking recipe, Jane says that a seance was in order for her ESP book. So she went about setting up Christmas tree lights and making other preparations. She got her money's worth; Seth stunned them. He transmogrified her body. It wasn't exactly a thing of beauty, to be sure, but it was a supernatural intervention. Not a high-order miracle, mind you, but it was something. Those at the table were told by the voice to concentrate on Jane's arm. One witness, Robert Butts, said that the hand began to change in appearance and resembled a paw. It gave Butts a very eerie feeling. He said that the hand became stubby and fat for a moment. Then it resumed its pawlike appearance. Then Seth told him to reach out and touch the hand. Butts cautiously touched Jane's hand. It felt very cold, wet, and clammy, and seemed unusually bumpy. Then Seth made the whole forepaw glow.

But as if this gesture was not enough, Seth had another trick. They faced a mirror and Seth told them to look at their reflections in the mirror. As they watched, Jane's image was replaced with another different image. The head dropped lower and the shape of the skull and the hair style changed. The head in the mirror leaned down although Jane was sitting erect, looking straight ahead. Naturally, it would take the three people a little while to acclimate themselves to such bizarre antics, but they would soon triumph and transcend their visceral horror.

The Seth sessions continued. The next breakthrough in the taking over of Jane's body was the appearance of a deep masculine voice, which issued from the medium's body. Seth told Jane's husband that he had been an extremely vain woman in a former life. Seth was also calling Jane "Ruburt," a male name. Then Seth commented philosophically that he feared that Jane would sound rather unmelodious as a man's voice.

Jane (now Ruburt) observed that they didn't realize they would receive what was known as the Seth material through the "psychic structure." She acknowledged a sense of great power in Seth's voice. It made her feel very small, as if surrounded by great energy. In time she would walk, gesture, and grimace while in a deep trance. She would even learn to sip wine occasionally as Seth spoke through her.

But there was an incident that almost ended the sessions. Jane, who by now had had a series of out-of-the-body experiences, said she was in her bedroom, and became suddenly aware of a dark, looming figure menacing her. She had not previously believed in demons, but changed her mind when the attacker dragged her around and even bit her hand. Finally the thing tried to kill her and she screamed.

Later, Seth would explain it all away. Naturally, it was merely a projection of her mind, the energy of hidden fears. Then Seth assured her and her husband [who took notes of everything the medium said} that the evil that "Ruburt" imagined did not exist.

Later, a fairly well-known psychologist interviewed Seth to see if it was a double personality. It was his opinion that Seth had a "massive intellect" and did not seem to be a secondary personality. Later this would be borne out clearly by a number of telepathic and clairvoyant tests, combined with the fact that the Seth creature would produce five thousand typewritten records and analogues of higher esoteric truth.

Some of it was most subtle, indeed, but much of the teachings would be a redundant weaving of semantic spells, as Seth came out again and again with the same ideas in different words. Invariably it would be in abstract, often abstruse, erudite, elusive language, with as much scientific and technical jargon as possible.

In this aspect, and in many of the teachings, the Seth material would be very similar to the impersonal voice that spoke through the entranced Edgar Cayce. Only at the end of Cayce's life, according to private sources, did the medium suspect that it was a powerful being and not the universal mind, the "Akashic records." Cayce's books have filled the book racks for twenty years, many of them best sellers for the past decade. He, like Arthur Ford, has been called "the greatest medium of the century."

But now back to Seth. Let's examine a number of these teachings. Jane Roberts reports on Seth's concept of God. Certain salient points of the description are:

1. God is not human, though he passed through human stages (and it is at this point that the Buddhist myth comes closest to approximating reality).

2. He is not a single individual, but an "energy gestalt."

3. This energy forms all the universes. Seth renames God "All That Is," as opposed to the "I Am That I Am" of the Holy Bible.

Creation, Seth says, was a massive dilemma for God and his one means of escape from cosmic insanity. This is exactly the opposite of the picture of joy, glory, and sovereignty of the biblical creation. In this case, "god" comes across as a huge tapeworm with a billion latent eggs. If the eggs do not spew out, the god will burst. The prototypes of creation, latent within its imagination, needed expression.

4. No personal God-individual exists, to use Christian terms. Human beings are cocreators, and what we call God is the sum of all consciousness, and yet the whole is more than the sum of its parts.

Seth stresses reincarnation time and again throughout the book, along with the God-is-within concept. If some of this is beginning to sound like science fiction with "Zonar Nine-Five" and "The folks from Astroid Twelve," or the U.S.S. Enterprise of "Star Trek" fame drifting along the cranial nerve of a billion-mile cretin, there is more to come. And this, I must admit, I find repugnant. If Frank Withers, the number-one spirit, was jettisoned and engulfed by Seth, something came along named Seth II, an ancient friend of Seth I, that gave Seth I a punt, as though he were a small soccer ball. (It reminds me of the cartoon of the ocean where the minnow is eaten by the bigger fish, and so on until the predator reaches the size of a sperm whale.) Seth II sounds like a large manta ray.

Ruburt (Alias Jane Roberts) tells what happened one night in April 1968 [the fifth year of the Seth sessions). By then Jane had been forbidden by Seth to read "religious books" and, as she confesses, she knew almost nothing about the Bible to begin with.

With massive power the voice started to break through, and Jane was hurled off into a void. The voice sounded clear though distant. Jane felt as if a cone had come down over her head. The voice claimed to come from an alien dimension, so alien that the contact was almost a miracle.

On June 8, the pyramid effect started again. Now it was plural, speaking of itself as "we." "They" described themselves as an entity which existed before our own time frame, and which was instrumental in forming energy into physical form.

Jane said that under this new Seth's influence, her body became like a puppet and her face expressionless.

After that visitation, Jane encountered difficulty getting back, and Seth had to help her.

When Jane went back into a trance, she had a trauma. Recently she had been not only the recipient of words, but of direct spiritual revelations and experiences as well. She says that the entity referred to individuals returning in the future to peer into physical reality like giants upon the floor. At that point she saw a giant's face peer into her living room, its face filling up the entire window. Then her body, the room, and its contents all grew to enormous size. She screamed and began to tremble violently.

Jane had one more bout with the higher Seth, but she became so shaken that the regular Seth did not allow it to continue for a long time. Again she felt the "cone" above her head and saw the giant looking at her. At this point she struggled to get in touch with her vocal cords. She seems to have felt somewhat violated by the being, a problem she never felt with the lower Seth. All the same, the medium goes on to make excuses for it, saying that it did not understand from its heightened state that she found the experiences unpleasant.

The last statement from Seth II in the chapter is a godlike declaration. He (or "they") claimed to have given man the mental images from which man formed the known world and his own physical self.

"Ruburt" has gone on to be with Seth, and newer channels have come on the scene to replace Jane Roberts (Ruburt). New entities have in turn replaced Seth—such as "Ramtha" and "Lazaris"—who feature among the bright new stars of Shirley MacLaine's autobiographies such as *Out on a Limb* and *Dancing in the Light*.

These newer entities have arrived with exquisite timing to a world in waiting. The advance work has been done. Unlike Seth, who only muttered in dark rooms before a handful of observers, other entities have spoken before millions. Compared to Seth, they have achieved superstar status.

The media have mentioned the enormous gate fees of these entities and their channels, an indicator of the surging popular interest. J.Z. Knight, who channels Ramtha, "on an average weekend draws up to 700 participants at $400 apiece ($280,000); she admits to earning millions of dollars from 'Ramtha,' "[1] and James Von Praagh quickly surpassed that.

The Entities

A pluralistic entity taking over a man in the Bible is seen in the madman, the Gadarene, whose name was Legion. Christ could have hurled the demons into the abyss; but as an illustration of their concrete reality, he sent them into a large herd of pigs. Then the pigs charged into the sea and killed themselves. The man in his possessed state had exhibited a sufficient range of superhuman and paranormal feats to scare everyone away. Among other things, he had the physical strength to snap heavy chains. But when Christ appeared, the demons trembled in horror. Legion was demon-possessed.

What is Seth? It—they, the pluralistic entity—is a demon, a mediumistic demon. There is no reason to believe what it says, for it is a brilliant liar. This woman's Ouija board caught a spiritual manta ray, and she is too seduced by it to know it. Yet Roberts is only too accountable, for at a specific time in her life she turned her back on the God of the Bible. She refers to that era scornfully, making sure to give us the caricatures. She says that as she grew older she found it increasingly difficult to accept the God of her ancestors. God seemed to be as dead as they were. And here comes the caricature, as she asks somewhat rhetorically what kind of God would require constant adoration by subjects sitting around singing hymns. This woman, who claims to be intelligent, asks this on the one hand and confesses ignorance of the Bible on the other hand.

Roberts made her decision. She decided that that kind of God was out and she would not have him as her friend. She then observes that it appears that God had not treated his own Son very well.

In the place of the biblical God, this woman has chosen the one who bears the same name as the Egyptian god of evil, "Seth," the ancient twin of Osiris; Seth, whose image is caned in the dank, musty descending corridors of stone beneath the Valley of the Kings, whose huge stone colossi lean against the bulbous pillars of Karnak, a subterranean god from the ancient past of Egypt. This multiple identity, Seth, claims to have never been enfleshed. Little wonder; this being from the void existed before the foundations of our world. It floated across the ancient world, for it is a spirit; it has always been a spirit. And there are others.

We learn from the Apostle Paul that the originators and powers behind the ancient idols were "elemental spirits." In 1 Corinthians 10:19, 20 (Revised Berkeley), Paul says, "What then am I saying? That an offering to idols amounts to anything, or that the idol itself is anything? No, but that which they sacrifice, they are offering to demons and not to God" (italics added). This problem is reiterated in Deuteronomy 32:16, 17 (NASB) about the truth of idol worship: "They sacrificed to demons who were not God, to gods whom they have not known, new gods who came lately." Such is Seth.

Again Paul says,' 'But the Spirit [of God] explicitly says that in later times some will fall away from the faith, paying attention to deceitful spirits and doctrines of demons" (1 Tim. 4:1, NASB). So there is dire warning to those who are already Christians. What will be the means of spiritual seduction? Deceitful spirits. Incidentally, the word demon, from the Greek daemon, means "knowing" or "wise." Spirits have knowledge far beyond mere temporal mortals, and the fierce range of their superhuman powers emerges when one studies the Greek connotations of the following words: *principalities*, powers, dominions. Ephesians 6:12 says, "For we wrestle not against flesh and blood, but against principalities, against powers, against the rulers of the darkness of this world, against spiritual wickedness in high places." In the Revised Berkeley Version, the latter part of the verse reads, "the cosmic powers of this present darkness; against the spiritual forces of evil in the heavenly spheres."

If you decided to turn your back on the biblical God, entered into occult pursuits, emptied your mind, and surrendered to an invisible intelligence, to whom or what would you go? The clear answer is: to one of these above-named wicked potentates. Not Fred Jones, not Fletcher (the guide to Arthur Ford), or anybody else with some tame home-town name, but instead, a *demonic* being. The blanket warning that the Bible issues regarding all spirit contact now emerges as a profoundly sensible injunction. Should you care to gamble in this particular casino, the odds against you infinitely outweigh the grade schooler trying his luck at Caesar's Palace in Las Vegas.

The consensus of all evangelical Bible scholars, using clear exegesis, is that the deceased, the dead, cannot be contacted. God has created an impassable barrier. What are, in fact, being contacted in place of the sought-after human souls are some type of deceiving spirits masquerading as the deceased, some spirits out of the untold myriad for whom Tehom ("the abyss") was prepared before the foundations of our physical universe. The number of these spirits is great, this we know. A genius, humanly speaking, with a massive genealogical card file, encyclopedic memory, and an active imagination could fool most people at a seance. An immortal spirit with a superhuman intelligence would have no trouble fooling just about anybody who tried to engage it, especially if the contact, no matter how brilliant, disregarded the Bible. Men alone are no match for these things.

Part of the "con" is to get people to believe that they are sufficiently armored with their own minds and intuitions. They are not. The Rand Think Tank is not, even if you throw in the faculty of M.I.T., Harvard, Stanford, and the Ivy League, even if you unified their minds. Unlike the baleful powers, none of these men was around to witness the creation of galaxies and atoms. The account of the role of the angelic hosts was that they saw, and in some way participated in, God's sovereign act of creation (they "shouted for joy," lob 38:7). Those among these creatures who would later oppose God, whose natures would twist, would still retain, in a perverted form, much of their intellect, power, and knowledge. What hideous strength they have!

Therefore, it makes sense, in the biblical tradition, for God to forbid spiritism. Anything else would not be love. If a host of cosmic beings once rebelled, then God knows of it and lovingly warns us of it. We have seen the numerous statements of Moody, Kubler-Ross, Cayce, Bishop Pike, Dowling, and Roberts. We have seen that there is an invisible world of beings—spirits—that some people can contact. We have seen their teachings, and the similarity of these teachings, and the obsession, common among all the teachings, with Jesus Christ. We also have seen the mainline spiritualistic and spiritistic views of the afterlife: that it is a progressive, multi layered, and multidimensional spirit plane where all souls evolve. The physical body is an unpleasant shell to be jettisoned. Real happiness, we are told, only begins on the other side. The biggest prize of all, we are then assured, is the ultimate stage of spiritual evolution where one becomes a being of light. We are asked to accept these statements on faith. It is that simple; this is a religion and its high priests are the mediums. To accept its view, we are forced to ignore the Bible and finally say, "The Bible is wrong." At that point, one has believed the spirits.

We are forced to ask, as God himself seeks to reason with his people, "And when they say to you, 'Consult the mediums and the wizards who whisper and mutter,' should not a people consult their God? Should they consult the dead on behalf of the living?" Isaiah 8:19, NASB).

Nevertheless, we are under endless bombardment of the newest and sleekest prototypes of this ancient phenomneon—channelers and wizards who "whisper and mutter" who rise and fall almost like rock stars.

7

SpiritVoices: James Van Praagh

Standing before several hundred spectators at the largest New Age Occult bookstore in America, James Van Praagh claims to see a much larger audience—spirits that he alone can sense among the living people in front of him. In West Hollywood's incense-filled Bodhi Tree bookstore he throws out a name to the audience swarming him: "Did someone here lose someone named Frances?" A dark-haired woman jumps out of her chair. "My aunt!" she gasps.

Stepping closer to the woman, who turns out to be actress Ava Fabian, Van Praagh rattles off a series of accurate facts about her late Aunt Fran: her bout with cancer, the trouble she had walking during her final days, and the closet Fabian has just cleaned. "I'm always reorganizing that closet!" the actress sighs. "This lady," Van Praagh says, nodding toward her aunt's invisible spirit, "helps you out a great deal." The audience applauds, and Fabian's eyes tear up. "I was moved, absolutely," she says later.[1]

No one is really able to do an official background check on the spirits that speak through these pop mediums (the public is not interested in Biblical sanctions). No official agency can vet the real identity of the "spirits," nevertheless the multitudes still listen to things they cannot even see, pinning their hopes and beliefs on invisible speakers. If the channeler is putting it all on by speaking in various contrived intonations of spirit voices, the situation is almost the same. Listeners are still pinning their beliefs on an unknown "speaker," one who is not even honest in the most rudimentary sense. If that is not deception—whether channeling or miming—I don't know what is.

Modern mediums not only chirp and mutter as they did in ancient Babylon and Chaldea but now they write bestsellers and appear on the talk show circuit. Most rise and fall in popularity like contemporary rock stars.

The most recent to appear in the limelight is James Van Praagh, author of *Talking to Heaven: A Medium's Message of Life after Death* which was at the top of the *New York Times* bestseller list for months, selling 1 million copies. It has been Van Praagh's ticket to a host of TV appearances from Oprah Winfey to 20/20. Clearly, he relishes his moment in history.

Van Praagh claims to be "clairsentient," meaning he senses when spirits are in the room and feels their personalities. He is in the right place at the right time to inspire the masses, a time when even the Psychic Friends Network can prosper. Van Praagh assures millions that they will have ultimate hope and meaning with absolutely no price tag or moral constraints attached. Such New Age assurances often have the shallow expediency of fast food formulas. But there is enough there to pull public attention.

Van Praagh usually appears on TV wearing bright turtlenecks and an ethereal gaze. He echoes the usual eastern and spiritualist beliefs, from Karma and spirit helpers to the evolutionary journey of the soul. But what endears him most with the public are his engaging tales of the spirit world. He gives them a proximity to the "other side" that they can almost reach out and touch.

Then there is his style. Van Praagh converses with the spirit world with the gossipy familiarity of a groupie at some Hollywood studio champaign and cheese party. It is casual, intimate, matter of fact, and long gone is any sense of horror with the supernatural. He also has an odd presence of his own. On the one hand James Van Praagh has the looks of a stocky bar tender, but he shatters this image the minute he speaks for out comes the overly saccharine voice of Richard Simmons, a disconcerting incongruity. Shades of the gay subculture. Women love it, most men look nervous or turned off.

When he is "on" Van Praagh doesn't go into trances but can be casually talking to someone one moment then suddenly speak on behalf of a spirit lurking nearby, all as a part of normal conversation.

A dead boyfriend can be giving his surviving girlfriend roses from the spirit world. Van Praagh says that the man is deeply sorry—we wonder what went wrong—as he mimics handing her roses. The camera shows a young woman in paralyzing anguish while Van Praagh is giving her invisible roses in the sweetest voice imaginable. This further breaks her. The camera leaves her trembling in tears. And James Van Praagh moves on. He has scored a clear "hit" as they say in the psychic trade, and it is on prime time television. This will sell books and keep the Van Praagh media circus rolling.

Those in grief are vulnerable and emotional targets—-which is part of the trade. In his book, he writes about a father and boy killed in a plane crash. Left behind is a disheartened wife and mother who comes to Van Praagh to find answers. Van Praagh asks the woman "Do you know the name Roger."[2] Then with tears of excitement "She replied that Roger was her husband's name" (Van Praagh, pg. 54). Van Praagh, himself impressed by what has happened, asks the woman about a little boy. Again, the woman is frantic and tells Van Praagh that a year ago her husband (a pilot) and young son were killed in an unfortunate plane crash. Roger, the so-called spirit, tells Van Praagh that everything is all right and wish my wife "happy anniversary." Then Tommy, the young spirit child from the other world, says some things that only a child might; like "Mommy don't be scared. I'm here with Daddy!" (Van Praagh, pg. 55) and asks to have his Star Wars poster removed from his wall. Tommy then tells Van Praagh that "he's not really mad at Bobby (his brother) for taking his red shirt out of his second drawer and wearing it" (Van Praagh, pg. 55).

One especially intriguing story appears in the chapter on "Tragic Transitions." A couple visits Van Praagh to receive comfort after the death of their son "Steven." Both the Police and the couple knew that Steven was on drugs and believed he died of suicide. But detective Van Praagh becomes the sleuth to solving the ultimate "who done it?" With the parents at his side, Van Praagh receives communication from Steven. Van Praagh translates, "Steven is screaming at me, I didn't kill myself. It was Ronnie. Ronnie did it to me. I didn't kill myself!" (Van

Praagh, pg. 60). Ronnie is a supposed drug dealer whom Steven owed drug money. The parents then run off and tell these things to the police. Van Praagh concludes the story by stating that Ronnie was soon captured, put on trial, admitted his guilt "and is currently serving a life sentence in a state penitentiary" (Van Praagh, pg. 62). Case closed! Except for one thing, there is no way to immediately corroborate any of it because there are no real details. It is a fortune cookie reading in which readers will assume it is a real person but no one in their circle of acquaintances. Attempts to verify have been futile.

Though he savors the limelight, one senses that Van Praagh can hardly wait to retreat from public view as soon as the show is over, much like actors after the final curtain. They mop their faces, clean up, and hit the town filled with the nervous energy that it took to create an artificial persona. Now they can be "themselves." Van Praagh's outward calm feels fragile, something that at any time could crack; then his syrupy assurances to hosts of adoring and needy women can explode into shrieks of loud falsetto laughter (like the scene in *The Birdcage*). A kind of moment of divine mediumistic madness, screams right out of San Francisco's Castro on Halloween night, to let all the spirits out.

James Van Praagh is either a gifted con artist and mentalist (when he does not flop) or a man touched by dark forces, and critics stand on both sides of the argument. In either case, there are things in his past that have helped his present road show.

Background

James Van Praagh was born in 1959 and raised as a Roman Catholic in the environs of New York City where he attended Sacred Heart Catholic school in Queens, N.Y. His father was in theatrical stage design of mostly off Broadway plays. Growing up around the New York theater world doubtless gave Van Praagh a certain feel for the theatrical—the fame, the fortune, the dynamic between performer and audience, even the partying after the show.

At an early age, his fascination with the "unknown" led him to experimentation with Ouija boards, haunted houses, and fortune telling 8-ball. He and his friend Scott, "...experimented with the usual paranormal games that seemed to be part of growing up for most kids" (Van Praagh, pg. 8). Van Praagh, after having a prophetic vision about a car accident, was told by his teacher, a Catholic nun, that he was "one of God's messengers" (Van Praagh, pg. 4) and that God had given him a special gift.

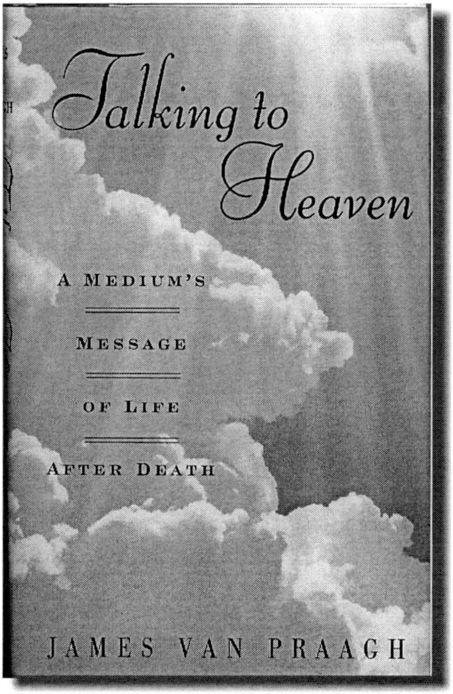

In 1982 Van Praagh attended San Francisco State College, while working on a degree in broadcasting. He was offered a position as a television writer to work in Los Angeles. After graduation, he returned to New York, packed his bags and made his way out to the city of "Angels." However, Van Praagh's job offer didn't pan out. Instead, something else happened in Los Angeles. He met a channeler named Brian who would forever change his life. Brian told Van Praagh that in two years he would be channeling spirits and would become quite popular.

Brian told him, "You know, James, you are very mediumistic. The spirit people are telling me that one day you will give readings like this to other people. The spirits are planning to use you" (Van Praagh, pg. 22).

Before Van Praagh's own bestselling book came out, he had spent several years working for the venerated William Morris literary Agency in New York City. It is the agency's business to hype manuscripts, sell authors to big houses, and look for subjects that will be hot in the marketplace. Undoubtedly this gave Van Praagh an edge on a marketplace already filled with New Age and mediumistic bestsellers. He might have even done a little rehearsing—or inventing—for his own moment on stage.

You cannot separate the medium and the message. His is New Age and spiritualistic all the way, an extension of every other pop medium to come on the scene.

Spirit Revelations

Van Praagh claims that he has had a direct revelation from God. "Although there was no booming voice of God to answer my real questions or reveal my destiny, I knew that the vision was God" (Van Praagh, pg. 7). Now convinced of God's existence, he began to pursue more actively the paranormal and was coerced by his mother to enter a Catholic Seminary. However, Van Praagh was dissatisfied with what he calls organized religion, and the Western *dualistic* notion of Heaven and Hell. He states, "all I knew is what I had been taught in Catholic school, and that was too one-sided" (Van Praagh, pg. 8).

After leaving seminary, Van Praagh could no longer believe in a Jesus, whom he saw replicated hanging on a cross, being the judge of the living and the dead. He presents Christianity in the familiar caricature as he explains, "I remember thinking: *How could someone like this make you burn in hell*?" (Van Praagh, pg. 15). He then decided that the traditional Christian view of God was too limited. He then made his leap into the realm of "higher consciousness" and pantheism.

God, for Van Praagh, is an energy that is everywhere and in all of us—"God is the creativity in all things. Each of us is perfect if we would only seek our divinity" (Van Praagh, pg. 27). The beautiful distinctions of the human race are reduced down to "holism." He states, "We are *all* the same. God has not chosen one group of people above another. (Van Praagh, pg. 84).

Van Praagh announces in a similar vein, "I believe we are all God… I am speaking not of our human qualities but of our spiritual qualities. Although we appear differently on the outside, we are all the same inside… We are all made of the *God Spark*." (p. 27) That is the core belief of all mysticism whether Indian, New Age, Theosophical or western occult. In the Upanishads, the term "*tat, tvam, asi*" (that thou art) announces that the true self is God. All eastern systems discuss death planes of various levels for various souls—the great ladder of being—that all traverse until they merge with the Godhead. *The Tibetan Book of the Dead*, the *Bardo Thodol*, as the primary example, enumerates endless realms for evolving souls. They are sent to a given plane or realm based on their earthly deeds, their karma. Then they are reborn. I believed this for years, above all, during my years in India. Van Praagh's version is more along the line of *Metaphysics for Dummies*. It is bone simple for the American public.

David Klinghoffer elaborates on Van Praagh's vision of heaven: "Mr. Van Praagh has learned many things from "God," aka spirits. There is a Heaven, and a Hell, the latter for individuals who have failed to love other people sufficiently. "Ultimately, we are all here to learn to love." Heaven is a very late-Nineties sort of place. There are spirits like "social workers or therapists" who help the recently deceased adjust to their new status. You can have a girlfriend or boyfriend up there if you want. There is no "judgment" or "prejudice," and spirits learn to "respect each other's uniqueness."[3] It sounds like a Whole Earth Expo teeming with New Agers and sensitivity training seminars.

Van Praagh puts into his vision a tiered system of heaven in which the "most developed" souls dwell in the highest levels. As for the immoral people of the earth, "they go to the heaven, or the hell, that they have created based upon their words, thoughts, and deeds while on earth." (p. 28) It is a decidedly Karmic system.

"Conveniently for his audience," Jon Carroll observes, "the heaven that Van Praagh talks to is relentlessly non-sectarian."[4] Van Praagh states in his book, "I must give appreciation to the 'Creative Expression' identified under various titles such as God, Allah, Yahweh, Divine Being, and Great Light. I will refer to this Power as the 'Source,' the Source of All."

There is one section devoted to his belief in yogic Chakra centers; the seven points on the human body where one can supposedly harness the energy of "god." He says, "as we meditate, our psychic centers are heightened because the stream of the Christ Consciousness that originates in the heart center flows through all the psychic centers, or chakras, of the body" (Van Praagh, pg. 182). There is the "root" chakra which gives one vitality. The "solar plexus" chakra which is the "seat of all intuition and psychic sensitivity" (Van Praagh, pg. 167). The "spleen" chakra which effects "our feelings, will and autonomy" (Van Praagh, pg. 167). Not to mention it enables a person to astral-travel. Then there is the "heart" chakra where the "higher spiritual elements of compassion, trust, giving, receiving, and nurturing are felt, and desire to serve people" (Van Praagh, pg. 168). The "throat" chakra which helps one to go under a hypnotic trance and be able to communicate with spirits. The "third eye" chakra which helps one to see the spirit people. And lastly, the "crown" chakra, located on the top of the head, is the "doorway to the higher or cosmic forces" (Van Praagh, pg. 168). Coming from India's different schools of yoga, this is nothing new to be sure.

There is a section on the "sixth sense" and a description of the four ways we can receive cosmic revelations. First, there is "clairvoyance," the psychic ability to see celestial visions. There is "clairaudience," the psychic ability to "hear sounds, names, voices, and music that vibrate on a higher frequency" (Van Praagh, pg. 32). The there is "clairsentience," or clear feeling, the psychic ability to feel paranormal things. Lastly, there is inspirational thought. "In inspirational thought, a medium receives thoughts, impressions, knowledge—all without forethought" (Van Praagh, pg. 32).

Van Praagh, borrowing heavily from the spiritualist movement, gives his own instructions to the public on how to become a spirit medium. There is a preparation guide on what one should eat. Then Van Praagh gives a list of psychic exercises. There is "psychometry," the meditation over sentimental objects. There is "automatic writing," allowing the spirits to write through a person. There are exercises that can be done through dreams and visions. And lastly there is the exercise of making a pact. This is where a person gets a spirit to tell them a sign or signal. For instance, one might get their spirit guide to have the traffic light blink green twice, just to confirm their authenticity. (Van Praagh, pg. 162)

Communing with animals

This is not to say that all of Van Praagh's work is derivative. In one area, at least, he can take reasonable pride in being a pioneer in the field. That would be the field of communication with dead pets.

In *Talking To Heaven* Van Praagh goes on to say that not only are we gifted with a divine inner light, but he has even found a way to talk to all of these creatures in heaven (if the dead, why not the living?).

Van Praagh describes his communications with departed pets. Some distraught over the death of a loved pet come to Van Praagh to hear from their animals. At this point, the pop medium has just gone beyond most contemporary mediums with an extra service. Pets communicate from heaven also, because as he states, "We are all made of the God *spark*. Even the lowest creature crawling on the ground is made from the same God *spark*" (Van Praagh, pg. 27).

Van Praagh describes how he got started in the dead pet world. One customer announced to him on hearing the name Charlie: "Yes! Charlie was my dog. Charlie is the one I came here to contact. He died two months ago, and I miss him very much." Van Praagh was taken back: "I could hardly believe what I was hearing. I realized why I was having trouble identifying a person. It became obvious that the information was *from the dog*! The dog was showing me things that he understood" (Van Praagh, pg. 134).

We are never told exactly how theses animals communicate with Van Praagh, we only know that Van Praagh could make millions in a nation so enamored with sweet assurances and willing to believe the Psychic Friends Network.

Reading the Crowd

A recent expose on ABC's 20/20 revealed some of the secrets behind Van Praagh's amazing "sensory" powers. At one point, a hidden camera saw Van Praagh ask a woman if her mother had died, and the woman replied that it was not her mother, but her grandmother. Van Praagh turned away and waited almost an hour before returning to the woman and revealing, "I want to tell you, there is a lady sitting behind you. She feels like a grandmother to me." Pumping audiences for information is only one of Van Praagh's gimmicks which we will examine later.

In an appearance on CNBC-TV's Charles Grodin Show, Van Praagh took a call from a man seeking to connect with his father, who it turns out was the actor John Wayne. Van Praagh was not told the man's identity except his first name. The call was prearranged by the network to test Van Praagh who did not exactly zero in on that famous cowboy drawl. This was his chance to mention on TV, "your father was the famous John Wayne and he says…" It was a clear miss. The medium then had to rationalize how he had failed, now resorting to the convenient language of the victim. Van Praagh explained the miss.

"(Setups) are done by people who have no understanding of mediumship or the properties of mediumship," Van Praagh said. "I would loved to have known that was John Wayne ... but you know, I'm only human, I don't hear it all the time."[5]

Van Praagh's book contains nothing about the long history of spiritualist charlatans and their varied techniques. It discusses spiritualist phenomena such as ectoplasm as a foregone fact as real as whooping cough or fog.[6]

Famed mentalists like Penn and Teller and "the amazing Randi" have mapped out the strategy of "how it is done." Other mentalists like Michael Shermer post articles on the internet exposing some of Van Praagh's methodology. Employing several trade secrets (often psychological gambits), Van Praagh uses any of three methods to dissemble conversations with "spirits from beyond."

The first is called the "cold read." Van Praagh's tool of choice, the cold read is when one person actually "reads" another, knowing nothing about the person. To read another human being is to ask that person various questions; to make statements, general and specific; and to observe the person's reactions to what is said. A nod of the head in the affirmative is the signal to proceed. From the most general clues, the reader may then move to more specific statements. When the reader discovers something, quite by accident, that he could seemingly never have known, he has made a hit. In most cases, it takes only a few such hits to convince the person being read of the sincere spiritual gifts of the reader.

The second of Van Praagh's techniques is an extension of the cold read known as the "warm read." The warm read takes advantage of normal human behaviors, for example, in mourning. A person mourning may wear certain jewelry that reminds them of a loved one, or keep a picture of that person in their wallet throughout the day. Recognizing these grief mechanisms, Van Praagh will ask someone if they have a memento from a loved one on them, and after receiving an affirmative nod Van Praagh will close his eyes, nod, and accept the duped person's praises. Confirming the fact that a death has occurred,

Van Praagh will then search for the cause of death by feeling either his head or his chest. If the person gives any feedback to either motion, Van Praagh will narrow the field by saying that he feels the death was sudden. This will elicit either an immediate reply in the affirmative or hesitation, in which case Van Praagh will back off and suggest a slower death. One might imagine that all of these incorrect guesses would warn the audience of Van Praagh's methods, but it requires only a few lucky hits to remove skepticism from an audience.

The "hot read" is the third technique and while it may be the most costly and time-consuming, if correctly used, the hot read can yield the most bountiful harvest of all the methods. In the hot read, the medium enters the session knowing something supposedly secret about his subject. Consider what a gifted hacker can find about almost any given person on the Internet—financial, criminal and medical records, even deeply personal information. With known personalities there is a wealth of information. Could that have been why Van Praagh was much more successful with Katie Couric on The Today Show, or Barbara Walters than various nameless faces in the crowd. Most in show biz have large publicity bios already available, indeed, bestselling biographies are not unusual.

Producers from the NBC show *The Other Side*, on which Van Praagh appeared numerous times early in his career, attest to his probing them for information backstage about people on the show, information which he miraculously divined later when the cameras were rolling.

Serving the spirit of the Age, Van Praagh goes beyond the usual stage tricks of mentalists. He teaches, seduces and entertains. He also makes a lot of money. In a non judgmental age as this, he is almost immune to criticism. And even if he were to be scandalized, the public would soon forget. What a time to be a medium.

Spiritual Dreamweaving

Van Praagh puts his own twists on the gospel removing it from the historic confines of orthodoxy and contradicting it with his own higher and deeper inspiration: "It was inside me. It spoke in my heart—not words, but feelings of an incredible love that God had for me and of which I was a part. I understood then that this feeling of god was not just found in a seminary or church but everywhere and in everything.

God is unlimited" (Van Praagh, pg. 19). With this universal God will come the suggestion that Christ is merely a higher master. Van Praagh narrates, "Nancy (a client) asked what I meant by the "Christ light of love," and I explained that it is *a pure, non judgmental love* of the highest caliber that was embodied by the master known as Jesus" (Van Praagh, pg. 113). It contradicts the gospels, but if it feels right, people will buy it.

Like so many contemporary voices in our time favored by the media, James Van Praagh comes across as nicer than God, more humane and accepting than God and would never judge people or nations as the Biblical God. This alone endears him with the public. In America today, no one wants to hear about the consequences of sin. That's all part of the old paradigm to be buried in history as quickly as possible.

Van Praagh chirps these false assurances to the masses often repeating the non judgmental motif of this permissive God, "God [is] love and non judgment, understanding and compromise… It [is] not the God who sat on a throne in heaven or the son of God who hung on a cross." (p.19). Indeed, it is very much a different god from the Biblical God. His god is more along the lines of Dionysus or the pagan gods of witchcraft.

And the consequences of sin—how does he deal with the cause and effects of sin?

Van Praagh takes one step further from center when he proclaims that AIDS is, on one level, a disease of the body, but on another, higher, level, it is the result of the spread of "hatred, prejudice, and intolerance." (p.84) Notice, it is not predominantly spread by the sinful acts themselves, but the intolerance concerning such acts that causes AIDS. This convoluted schema is a perfect example of the biblical admonition against those who call evil good and good evil.

To Van Praagh AIDS is also a kindergarten morality lesson, "because of AIDS we are being forced to learn lessons of tolerance, understanding, and acceptance." (p.85). Really? Clearly this is on behalf of the homosexual and lesbian minority and the medium is using the spirit world to justify them. At root is a war on biblical morality.

Van Praagh finishes the concluding paragraph of *Talking To Heaven* with the assuring words that his readers are all gods. "You put on the robe as a reminder that you are invincible. **You are truly Gods.**"

It's maybe too sweet and sounds hollow in the end.

God's Tough Love

In Genesis 2: 14. It was promised the ancient hearers that they too would become like gods. Unfortunately it was the serpent that made the promise, not God. It was the god of this world, the spirit behind sin and depravity. And he will talk through any unholy conduit he can.

What of the true God, the biblical God. Does he really warn against what James Van Praagh is doing? And if Van Praagh is in opposition to God with his acts, is it then any wonder that his teachings are in equal opposition to God?

Indeed, God has intervened in history, and the Bible is the record of that intervention. Man did not just perform some religious rite and summon so great a One as God into speaking. Rather, God himself purposed his communications in his own way and on his own terms, which has always been a problem to many.

The Bible says many many things. But about what Van Praagh is doing, the Bible judges such mediumship as detestable. It also notes that you cannot any more sit at a seance and summon Uncle Rex than you can dip a fishing pole into the water at Dover, England, and pull in the same little gray fish you would if you fished in Miami. "But it looks the same." Indeed it does. The entities are not the deceased, they are not who they claim to be.

The occult threat of the depraved practices of the Canaanites was so great, its intermixing with God's truth so abhorrent, that God warned about it severely. We have to take on faith the fact that the Creator would know why.

Consider the ways the Bible unmasks the practice of mediumship in the following passages.

Sometimes it begins by asking a reasonable question:

> And when they say to you, 'Consult the mediums and the wizards who whisper and mutter,' should not a people consult their God? Should they consult the dead on behalf of the living? (Isa. 8:19).

Beyond that, what happens to those who go to mediums?

> Do not turn to mediums and wizards; do not seek them out, to be defiled by them: I am the Lord your God (Lev. 19:31, RSV).

The result? People become *defiled*.

Sometimes God issues a warning that involves judgment as the consequence:

> If a person turns to mediums and wizards, playing the harlot after them, I will set my face against that person, and will cut him off from among his people (Lev. 20:6, RSV).

And to show the full scope of the horror, God offers the death penalty to spare his entire people from being defiled as a race and destroyed:

> A man or a woman who is a medium or wizard shall be put to death; they shall be stoned with stones, their blood shall be upon them (Lev. 20:27, RSV).

When Saul went to a medium, the witch of Endor, that single visit alone was a great enough disobedience in the face of God's repeated warnings to Saul for him to forfeit his kingship to King David. Just one brush with a medium brought terrible judgment upon Saul.

Has God changed his mind about going to mediums now that Van Praagh and countless other sweet talking mediums walk the earth? Only if God's nature can change and be assure that that cannot happen.

While God warns of the consequences, James Van Praagh boasts of having a séance at the Hollywood United Methodist Church. "I could not believe I was doing a séance in a church. I laughed to myself and thought, *Ha, if only my family priest could see me now!*" (Van Praagh, pg. 104).

Why does God address the reality of mediumship and familiar spirits in such harsh language? Because beneath the calm surface of this occult venture lurks terrible danger for those who dabble. Let's bring home the point with a human analogy.

Consider yourself in the position of a parent trying to impress a child with the dangers of picking up an adder or a black widow spider—something that can kill with a single bite. The stakes are enormous. The young child can die in a brief instant with no further chances at life, an all-or-none proposition with deadly consequences. The small child can not possibly appreciate the reasons for such severe language at the time—perhaps a red faced parent screaming at them at top volume. God deems the spiritual danger of mediumship to be equally serious. The situation warrants language of equal severity as a parent warning a child about a deadly snake bite.

For a nation who *en mass* have embraced Saul's deadly blunder many times over in the public arena—seeking after mediums—this does not bode well. America at the end of the twentieth century evidently would prefer to hear the voice of a lisping medium over that of God. No one wants to hear the suggestion that James Van Praagh's sweet assurances are closer to some character in a Stephen King novel—perhaps the operator at an amusement park roller coaster ride who lisps sweetly while guiding the screaming kids into some abyss while grinning hideously in the process.

8

The Seat of The Soul: Gary Zukav

"Let Go. Trust. Create. Be who you are. The rest is up to your nonphysical Teachers and the Universe. Take your hands off the steering wheel. Be able to say to the Universe, 'Thy will be done,' and know it within your intentions."[1]—Gary Zukav

Some, like Gary Zukav, can make millions in today's world by promoting the latest hot views in the cultural arena—New Age, politically correct, pro-feminist, anti-traditional all entwined as a package. People eat it up. It's the truth that's become an embarrassment. God—the Biblical God—has been relegated to a distant place in line by the present genre of media barons and thinkers.

God is not even allowed to voice a timid objection in today's savvy realm of the media. Imagine, if it were possible, God holding up his hand in some talk show audience asking, "Can I say something?" to loud jeers. If this scenario were possible most of today's talk shows from Oprah to Jerry Springer would not call on Him. He would get no voice. This is certainly the case for those who represent Him on the earth—the real ones! His people are in the back of the audience, voiceless or ridiculed.

When the media portrays one of God's "representatives," a "Christian," they make sure to find someone who resembles the well established caricature of a wide eyed, ignorant, cult follower who is barely coherent, volatile, and ready to go off at the sound of a twig snapping. Such characters constantly appear on TV shows and in the movies, inevitably, ugly to the core and a danger to society.

Usually these "Christians" portrayed in the media hear voices, have a big glowing cross on a trailer wall and a huge carving knife on the wall next to it. It's amazing how many serial killers in the movies are seen surrounded with crosses and other Christian memorabilia. This type of secular mockery works amazingly well in tandem with the Christian subculture forever shooting itself in the foot. On the other side of this dark picture we see ranting TV preachers either caught in scandal or begging for money like con artists. Their TV teachings debilitate the integrity of the church with easy promises of health and wealth and quick escapes from suffering. If hard times come, it seems inevitable that many will fall away feeling abandoned by God.

The Christian Faith that was once noble has become a sideshow carnival. While growing numbers of the "sheeple" can't seem to tell the difference or don't really care (they're preoccupied buying raffle tickets for guaranteed prosperity without trials or suffering with a place in line for an early exit into the clouds). The very brightest—including genuinely honest seekers—are increasingly turned off, defect or drop out.

As the public forum dispenses of Christianity, it can bring in New Age alternatives which seem so much more sophisticated, appealing, and broad minded than the "Christian fanaticism" the public sees portrayed. The only "reasonable" Christian voices allowed in the larger public forum are usually the ecumenical ones who have adapted the newest trends—their creed is compromised, syncretistic, politically correct, globalist, New Age. Inevitably, they are intelligent, articulate, and sophisticated. Bestselling author M. Scott Peck, a Harvard educated psychiatrist, is a good example of this phenomenon. His "Christian" writings trumpet global community and the communion of all spiritual paths. But the more conservative views keep moving from Christian marginalization to public taboo, indeed, criminalization. Christians, who are losing ground by degrees, can't see they are losing the culture war. The frog pot is heating up quickly—and the frog is licking its chops for the new soup.

The culture responds to those latest teachings seen on television: broad roads to unlimited power, pleasure and fun. Gary Zukav, one of the latest of the New Age phenoms, does indeed pump out the latest views into the cultural arena.

Publisher's Weekly reports that Zukav is "the first author featured in Oprah's 'Renew Your Spirit' segment the week of September 28, 1998; he did a series of five-minute spots over four days and the book shot up the lists. *Seat of the Soul* has had a total of 23 printings, seven since the Oprah show. Zukav again appeared on Oprah in December of 1998. Fireside shipped more than 320,000 copies to meet the demand; copies in print total about 700,000." Oprah continues to feature *Seat of the Soul* on her web site.

Without question, Zukav has entered the halls of favor where no Christian is allowed to tread. Indeed, his deception rides on a magic carpet. Before that Zukav published *The Dancing Wu Li Masters*. I used to see it prominently displayed at the Book Depot Bookstore Cafe in Mill Valley's town square when I came down from my residence in the hills (Zukav lives in the area and I am sure I have seen him in some Marin County cafe.). *The Dancing Wu Li Masters* won The American Book Award for Science and was given a rave review in the *New York Times* when it first came out. In Zukav's words, it has become the bible for those who are interested in learning about quantum physics, but who are not drawn to mathematics or science. Zukav's first book added to the work of New Age physicist, Fritjof Capra in synthesizing New Age beliefs with physics.

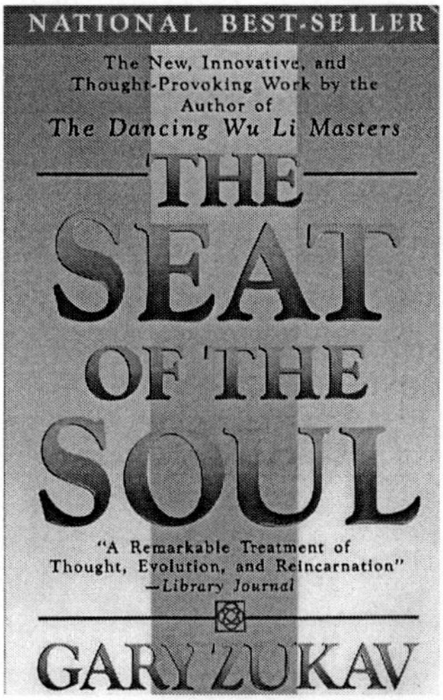

Now Zukav has moved to metaphysical speculations in *Seat of the Soul*. In truth, his definition of the soul is the Vedantic description of the *atma*. Like a lot of today's bestselling synthesizers of knowledge—Deepak Chopra being preeminent—Zukav simply updates ancient concepts with new metaphors. Countless bestsellers have been produced this way.

Let me make a frank confession as an author who has tried to break into the New York publishing establishment at various times—where publishing houses tower into the Manhattan sky, whose marketing engines are sometimes beyond belief. I have occasionally heard the voice of temptation goading me with, "Just go back to being a New Ager. The way you write, the New York publishing world will have your books all over the place. Stop fighting the system. The Christian houses can never reach the secular audience you want to reach. And have such a diminished down audience, your book will be out of print within a year."

Zukav should feel blessed with , his easy acceptance by the huge houses considering his modest talent as a writer.

Zukav is also a zealot, ever busy with global concerns. He not only writes but he passionately promotes his beliefs as an activist (another lesson for Christians waiting in passive indifference before they leave this world). Zukav is a member of numerous organizations and activities, among them: the Club of Budapest, World Business Academy, Native American Earth Ambassadors, CoCreate with the Earth Foundation, EarthSave, and the Intuition Network. He has also been on the advisory board for Earth Day 1990, the chair of the Government and Politics Strategy Group for the Campaign for the Earth. He sees a new world coming. And unfortunately, he may be right—-his new world may be heaven for some and a nightmare for others.

Zukav announces his mission as a social catalyst on his web page: "My life is dedicated to the birth of a new humanity. That birth is now in progress. We are all involved in it. The new humanity is being born inside us. We are awakening to new perceptions and new values. These are leading us to new goals." He continues, "Our new values are the values of the soul—harmony, cooperation, sharing, and reverence for Life. Our new goals are authentic power - the alignment of the personality with the soul—and a planet without conflict." Without conflict except for the unbending "old paradigm" believers who will have to be aggressively swept off the evolutionary highway to make way for the New World.

Now let me make another confession. I have often envied the sheer talent, imagination, and seemingly limitless resources of the ideological left. They have billions to our thousands and they spend it cunningly. They take risks and invest with passion—apparently believing in their cause more than we believe in ours—starting publishing empires, movie studios, syndicated TV networks, many of the Fortune 500 corporations, banking, and so on. Their foundations give colossal amounts of money to programs destined to change culture, from PBS specials to slick magazines and vocal social causes. They are far sighted and dedicated. They have a plan and we don't. We retreat from the world as they take over. And they are winning the culture war hands down. Nothing can stop them, for they seem to have the winds of history blowing behind them.

In the army of talent on ideological left, there are countless New Age voices. Gary Zukav is one of them, a small face in a very big crowd—passionate, talented, a true believer, like most of them. Many of them are graduates of the Ivy League and other privileged universities, and like Gary Zukav, are secularized Jews who are completely turned off by the

Christian alternative (Can they really bear to watch televangelist Robert Tilton twitching or can they really intellectually respect Jimmy Swaggart?). Their promised land has become the New Age, perhaps because it is like an emanation out of the Jewish Kabbalah. Among them are Ram Dass (Richard Alpert), Barbara Marx Hubbard, Stanoslav Grof, Stanley Krippner, Howard Rheingold, Judith Skutch, Margot Adler, George Leonard, Bernie Siegel, MD, Andrew Weil, MD, Marianne Williamson, and Brian Weiss, MD, to name a sample. Extremely bright and well placed, these are voices that steer our culture with barely a breath of resistance. America moulds obediently. You could say they are in the right place at the right time. And that includes Gary Zukav. Oh, to be a change agent in a post-Christian age, it's like cutting butter these days.

Gary Zukav had an important turning point in the mid-70's when he went to Esalen Institute at Big Sur, the spawning ground for high end New Age paradigms on anything from transpersonal psychology to physics. He came to Esalen as a journalist, not a scientist, brought by Jack Sarfatti. his room mate. They were living in North Beach, San Francisco. Zukav got the idea to write his first book, *Dancing Wu Li Masters*, at Esalen. Sarfatti, a physicist, allegedly wrote parts of it and guided Zukav on the physics. The term "Wu Li" was adopted for the book's title during a 1976 conference at Esalen on Physics and Consciousness, involving Zukav, Sarfatti, T'ai Chi Master Huang, and David Finkelstein, among others.

Countless visionaries of New Age and radical thought came through Esalen during that period from Tim Leary to Ram Dass, from Maslow to Eric Berne, a virtual Who's Who of intellectual catalysts. Zukav's time would come to advance the charge. And it did in the late 1980's.

Gary Zukav's latest bestseller, *The Seat of the Soul*, runs the Esalen torch of human potential into new territory, the evolutionary leap of the species from a "five-sensory" species that pursues external power (i.e., domination over the environment and other people) over to a "multi sensory" species that pursues "authentic power" of the spirit. Zukav tell the public that the soul is destined for greatness beyond the confines of traditional thinking and he shares the secret.

The Secrets of the Soul

Gary Zukav reveals that reincarnation is the hidden force that makes us the people we are. Our character traits come from many lifetimes. Yes, it's an idea that has been kicking around for a long time.

Zukav explains, "The lifetime of your personality is one of a myriad of experiences of your soul. The soul exists outside of time. The perspective of the soul is immense, and the perception of the soul is without the limitations of the personality. . . . For each incarnation, the soul creates a different personality and body.[2]" These words could have come from any number of gurus on the Hindu concept of the soul, the *atma*. "After an incarnation, the soul returns to its immortal and timeless state. It returns once again to its natural state of compassion, clarity and boundless love."

Our sojourn through the world is to evolve through the "earth school," Zukav's trademarked term reminiscent of Edgar Cayce's "earthplane." It is merely one plane of being, what the Hindus call a "*Loka*." *The Tibetan Book of the Dead*, would call it a "*Bardo*." Such concepts were first borrowed from Eastern thought by Edgar Cayce, the Rosicrucians, and the Theosophists (Annie Bessant, Alice Bailey, and Madame Blavatsky) among others.

Zukav describes the soul between lifetimes: "When the soul returns to its home, what has been accumulated in that lifetime is assessed with the loving assistance of its Teachers and guides." This is also the same deathplane scenario—encounters with Beings of Light—recycled in recent bestsellers by Betty Eadie and Dannion Brinkley.

Zukav describes the cosmic bookkeeping of the soul on the deathplane: "The new lessons that have emerged to be learned, the new karmic obligations that must be paid, are seen. The experiences of the incarnation just completed are reviewed in the fullness of understanding."[3] The process continues in the next incarnation, and so on.

Then he divulges the great dynamic of the soul: "The center of the evolutionary process is choice. It is the engine of our evolution."[4] We make ourselves and remake ourselves.

What were once called "sins" are really negative choices that create bad karma that must be overcome and counterbalanced by "right action" in order for the soul to evolve. We inevitably experience temptation along the way. If we resist such ignorance of choice (the Vedantic concept) then we short circuit what might become a painful lesson involving lifetimes of struggle. The cruel version of this—that I used to recite to myself the years I lived in India—is that a really bad action can reverse innumerable lifetimes of sustained virtue, forcing the "higher soul" to go crashing down to the base level of an insect, algae, or monster. New Agers all aglow with the possibilities of instant godhood miss this dark downward slope. A bad enough choice and you slide back to the evolutionary starting gate. It is all mechanics and no grace.

Zukav hints at this kind of fall when he says, "Great souls, such as the soul that was Gandhi, for example, run the risk of great contamination."[5] If they do not live up to their potential, then they can experience a huge loss. "As you look at the individuals who are in major positions of influence upon our planet you can see whether or not they are succeeding at their tasks of advancing humanity by the choices they have made. Some have chosen to align themselves, like mannequins, with . .. a system that is disintegrating..."[6] In other words, they are failing to implement the new paradigms. Or put another way, they are stalling at the gate of the New Age, clinging to old values.

Zukav mentions how temptation can be a gentle short cut. "Temptation is the Universe's compassionate way of allowing you to run through what would be a harmful negative karmic dynamic if you were to allow it to become physically manifest."[7]

Reminiscent of some of the thoughts of M. Scott Peck, Zukav comes up with a heavily psychologized "Me Generation" insight that those who have been fans of John Bradshaw's "recovery" seminars, would love. For a generation that loves good feelings and is forever redefining itself interpersonally, Zukav speaks of the ever popular subject of the temptation/addiction cycle: "If you decide that you cannot beat a temptation, what you are really doing is *giving yourself permission to be irresponsible.* The desires and impulses that you feel that you cannot resist, that you lack the power to overcome, are your addiction." To many in his audience, Zukav has scored a point. They can dwell on this "insight." It has that recovery group feel. And it may hold partial truth. Zukav's book has a number of such hooks—perhaps its most insidious power. There is an entire chapter on addictions: chemical, interpersonal, and sexual, which comprise the temptations of our age and its love of pleasure.

But temptations can reveal deeper secrets—Luciferic ones.

We learn that Lucifer has a positive and liberating role through temptation—far from the Bible's unfortunate portrayal of him where he has been misunderstood for ages. Zukav declares a kind of New Age year of Jubilee on this nemesis of the biblical God, giving him the same kind of positive reading that Madam Blavatsky and Annie Bessant of the Theosophical movement gave Lucifer; To them, Lucifer was the enlightener, bringing the knowledge of good and evil and hence freeing man to become God. It was a positive gift.

Zukav reveals the ancient tempter's service to humanity: "Lucifer means 'Light bringer.' Temptation, the *Luciferic principle*, is that dynamic through which each soul is graciously offered the opportunity to challenge those parts of itself that resists Light."[8] Like a good transpersonal therapist, Lucifer just shines light on our weaknesses so we can evolve.

And that brings up the nature of this Light that "the Light Bearer" brings. It is another secret. "Every physical form as well as every non-physical form *is Light* that has been shaped by consciousness. No form exists apart from consciousness. . . . Physical reality and the organisms and forms within physical reality are systems of Light within systems of Light, and this Light is the same Light as the Light of your soul."[9]

Lucifer the "light bringer" is therefore part of the enlightenment process.

But what about evil, is it real? Is evil a moral absolute? No. Zukav turns eastward again to say that evil is just our own creation. It is also a part of a dualistic universe—yin and yang—that we create, or at least cocreate.

"Hold onto the thought that you create your experiences. Your fear comes from the realization that a part of you is creating a reality that it wants."[10] Like the scene in the film, *What Dreams May Come*, the over-mind cocreates its own reality on-the-fly as the texture of outward reality changes to suit the will. If you are in a bad place, *you created it.* You are responsible, the agent of reality.

The problem of evil and suffering is therefore the earth school teaching the immortal soul lessons for its own evolution. "When we see a person sleeping in the gutter in the winter, we do not know what is being completed for that soul. We do not know whether that soul engaged in cruelty in another lifetime."[11] One woman at an early 80s Transpersonal psychology conference was told that on a karmic level she engineered her own rape.

In classical thinking, we say that if someone does something wrong and receives due punishment, he can easily recall the wrongdoing that brought the consequent punishment. It's immediate cause and effect and the lesson is obvious. If the evil action, the offense, was ten lifetimes back and the offender can't remember it, then his misfortune in this lifetime makes no sense because he cannot connect his retribution with the offense (its like punishing a dog a year after it chewed up the sofa—the dog won't have a clue what's going on.). The feedback between deed and resultant consequence is now moved to cover lifetimes. So in almost all cases with this schema, the present life is a dilemma that makes no sense. Therefore there is no way to learn the cosmic lesson—-and the cosmic lesson is completely lost. Zukav makes the argument that the Soul, on the higher plane, does remember. So the "personality" operates in the dark "intuitively" until it is more connected with the soul.

The biblical view is simply that cause and effect are in constant operation, and that makes a fallen world even more tragic. There are real consequences for evil actions and they are not illusory. This also makes sense of the inevitability of judgment. If someone decides to murder another person, the offender might be able to get away with it for a while, but there is a genuine victim—real losses—and the perpetrator has the person's blood on his head. Beyond the temporal judgment of the state—which can be uneven and unjust—there is still the judgment of a Holy God. Sin implies that moral laws are eternal standards set by a transcendent God and that the individual who sins has moral agency. The Biblical escape route from eternal judgment is the profound mystery of the Grace of God through Christ. The mission of Christ if fundamental.

But Zukav's spin feels great on the surface to those who love doing their own thing.

Morality comes from the self according to Zukav. "Karma is *not* a moral dynamic. ***Morality is a human creation.*** The Universe does not judge. The law of karma governs the balancing of energy within our system of morality and within those of our neighbors. It serves humanity as an impersonal and Universal teacher of responsibility."[12] What we have are not the biblical laws of morality, right and wrong, based on absolute standards coming from a transcendent personal God, but the laws of Karma from an impersonal godhead.

So the lesson from all this according to Zukav is not to judge. "When we judge, we create negative karma. Judgment is a function of the personality. . . . When we say of an action, 'This is right' or 'that is wrong,' we create negative karma."[13]

Christ is then manipulated into the argument by Zukav to support the thesis never to judge the rightness or wrongness of an action. "The Christ did not judge even those who spit in his face, and who subjected Him without mercy to His pain and humiliation. He asked forgiveness, not vengeance, for those who tortured him. Did neither the Christ nor Gandhi know the meaning of justice? They knew non judgmental justice."[14]

But there is a serious problem here with Zukav's non judgmental Christ. Christ indeed judged his generation numerous times, which is what got him into trouble with the religious establishment of his day, both Pharisees and Sadducees, just like his predecessor John the Baptist ("Ye generation of vipers" John told them.). Jesus indeed pronounced woes on evil doers, warning of impending judgment repeatedly. He drove the money changers out of the temple with a whip. And he spoke of the grim consequences of sin. Why? To prevent sin and its consequences by alerting his generation of his real mission. They utterly missed the point, waiting for a messiah king to trash the Roman occupation.

On lesser levels, we warn about the consequences of sin daily. Some call it tough love. It happens in healthy families day in and day out. "Son, if you drive back from the party drunk, you could have a head on collision on the highway and die." The warning is so the event won't happen, a preventative based on genuine concern. Zukav's journey is fairly free of warnings.

The Great Journey

The rare initiate moves past plane after plane by heroic and difficult acts. The secret is the divine *gnosis*, the secret knowledge given the adept. It's all a giant labyrinth. Zukav borrows the imagery of Carl Jung for this ascendance through Gnostic realms. To Jung, all these realms lay within the Self as archetypes. The process of joining them through progressive illumination Jung called "individuation."

Zukav reveals the Gnostic aspect of the earth school. The Gnostics emphasized leaving the dense realm of matter to ascend into the realm of the spirit. Zukav says that "aspects of your soul that need to interact in physical matter in order to be brought into wholeness."[15]

After reading Zukav for a while you realize that it's like a weekend marathon at Big Sur, as he weaves ideas coming from Fritz Perls, Abraham Maslow, Eric Berne, and a host of other Esalen gurus who formed the bridge to transpersonal psychology.

Zukav instructs this generation on the hidden mechanics of the soul's journey towards godhood.

Reincarnation, spoken of earlier, is part of the broader concept of transmigration. A soul is reborn not just through human bodies, but where the "consciousness" moves up "the scale of being" from lowly mineral to animal, to human and beyond to the godhead. This is the foundation of Hinduism.

For a moment, Zukav puts on the Shaman's mask informing us that animal species are possessed by a "group soul." There is a single group soul "of enormous impersonal energy that is called 'buffalo.' It is an enormous expansive sphere of impersonal energy that is called buffalo consciousness."[16] Unlike science, he does not need to prove a thing, he can shoot from the hip.

How does Zukav account for an animal graduating to the human level? "What of an animal that lays down its life for its human? . . . That, for an animal, is graduation to the human experience, or to its next higher level."[17] In soul points he rates the Dolphin twenty percentile points above the dog, and so on (Van Prague might be interested in this).

He adds, "The journey toward individual soulhood is what distinguishes the human kingdom from the animal kingdom, the vegetable kingdom and the mineral kingdom. Only the human kingdom has the experience of individual soulhood. That is why its powers of creation are great. The soul process moves through degrees of awareness."[18] We evolve from five sensory to multisensory.

"Reincarnation and the role of Karma in the development of the soul will be central parts of *spiritual psychology*."[19] Zukav claims that "Spiritual psychology" will show that, "if your soul was a Roman centurion, an Indian beggar, a Mexican mother, a nomad boy, and a medieval nun, among other incarnations, for example, and if the karmic patterns that were set into motion within those lifetimes are in motion within you, you will not be able to understand your proclivities, or interests, or ways of responding to different situations without an awareness of the experiences of those lifetimes."[20] The secret is past life recall.

But we must move on with the soul journey.

There are states on the scale beyond human. At some point one's soul "chooses to learn in the nonphysical realm. It may choose to learn through the task of becoming a nonphysical guide. . . Beyond that comes the experience of master, the experience of moving into advanced levels of Light that is no longer specific to human. Our nonphysical Teachers are from these levels of Light."[21]

Even planets are on the same ladder seeking higher consciousness. The earth itself is composed of other merging consciousnesses "that we call countries societies and nations." Nations are aspects "of the personality of Gaia, the Earth's soul, which itself is developing its personality and soulhood."[22]

The earth, as Gaia, "has agreed to interact with the human species, and to allow the development of this species to merge with its own consciousness. Part of this agreement can be understood as an agreement that matter will be cocreated upon this planet with the consciousness of the Earth. Since the Earth now has creative residents, it responds to their energy. Our species and the Earth form a mutual response system."[23] Note that this also has ecological undertones along with goddess undertones since Gaia is the ancient goddess. Zukav's cosmic tapestry continues.

Beyond gods, angels and planetary consciousness the journey moves into pure light. Zukav admonishes that we are light. "The Light that flows through your system is Universal energy. It is the Light of the Universe. You give that light form."[24]

"Every physical form as well as every nonphysical form is Light that has been shaped by consciousness. No form exists apart from consciousness. . . . Physical reality and the organisms and forms within physical reality are systems of Light within systems of Light, and this Light is the same Light as the Light of your soul."[25]

When Light awakens to its divine nature at the end of the journey, it realizes its supreme identity, to borrow a book title by Harvard Orientalist Alan Watts. Zukav invokes the timeless Hindu metaphor of the drop returning to the ocean after the long journey through *Samsara*:

"You have always been, because what it is that you are, is God or Divine intelligence, but God takes on individual forms, droplets, reducing its power to small particles of individual consciousness.... As the little form grows in power, in selfhood, in its own consciousness of self, it becomes larger and more Godlike. Then it becomes God."[26]

Till this time comes, we must make do with the Earth School. And that means relationships with other people, five-sensory and multi sensory. And here is where the Oprah Winfrey crowd start to feel good. Because though everyone wants to become God as soon as possible, this is a way off. But relationships can be around the next corner.

Beyond Marriage

Some of the sound bytes from Zukav's book seem custom crafted to cause moments of awe when pronounced sagely on such shows as Oprah Winfrey. He covers America's hottest topics—**empowerment** and **relationships**. And as this culture continues to deconstruct, the most saccharine promises about true relationships and personal power will warm any needy audience.

We live in the time of the lone predator, people using people with little loyalty and even less longevity of relationship. Then there is the healing after the cohabiting is over. Healing and public confession. Of course the latter is more geared to Sally Jesse Raphael. Jerry Springer's show goes more for the out and out event horizon of the post human—an air balloon wedding over Borneo between a human and a Chimpanzee timed at the moment a rocket takes off with someone waiting for a space alien as a soulmate, and so on.

America has turned into a singles culture—many formerly married are now divorced, others are simply cohabiting till the thrill is gone. As such, America is post family. We have multiple divorces, single parents and, unfortunately, homosexual "marriages" and adoptions. All these rotating relationships are even more short lived. The result is the single image on TVs hottest new program, *Ally McBeal.* She walks alone. So does our culture. At such times, people need assurance. And Zukav gives assurance in the evolutionary sense. Some of it comes out as a word salad of elaborate psychobabble. I'll let him say it: "Spiritual Partnerships."

Zukav announces the end of marriage, disappearing with the Old World Order and its traditional views. It is old paradigm, and therefore, part of the problem. "Just as external power is no longer appropriate to our evolution, the archetype of marriage is no longer appropriate." Then he cautions, "This does not mean that the institution of marriage will disappear overnight . . . " Though many hope it will disappear as soon as possible, because then new freedoms can begin, starting with a constant round robbin of "relationships." In comes the new, out goes the old. If a partner becomes spotty, trade 'em in for a new model. Esalen was pioneering this ground over two decades ago. It is amazing how many New Age therapists have been changing partners.

Instead of marriage, "spiritual partnerships" no longer have a man and woman becoming one flesh, but people (they love the word "persons") entering alliances for mutual evolution. "Spiritual partnership is a much freer and more spiritually accurate dynamic than marriage because spiritual partners come together from a position of spirit and consciousness"[27] (so all those wedding vows consecrated before God by Christian believers are not conscious or spiritual according to Zukav).

This high sounding paradigm is described: "The bond between spiritual partners exists as real as it does in marriage, but for significantly different reasons. Spiritual partners are not together in order to quell each other's financial fears or because they can produce a house in the suburbs and that entire conceptual framework. . . . . The commitment of spiritual partners is to each other's spiritual growth, recognizing that that is what each of them is doing on Earth, and that everything serves that."[28]

Under different rules than marriage, such partnerships can have high turnover rates. "The duration of their partnership is determined by how long it is appropriate for their evolution to be together."[29] Another key word, "evolution." The really fast evolvers can play a kind of musical chairs. "We have ceased to evolve" will probably replace older excuses for divorce.

Nevertheless, "commitment" another magic word for these relationally minded people, even for high turnover situations. "Without commitment, you cannot learn to see others as your soul sees them—as beautiful and powerful spirits of Light."[30]

"Commitment" has also been the high sounding rationalization for "domestic partnerships," the model that has replaced conventional marriage, starting in the San Francisco Bay Area where the "gay subculture" is looking for tax breaks, insurance benefits and legitimacy. Each relationship can define what "committed" means and how long it will last. Often, such "relationships" are defined on the fly and can end quickly. In the homosexual subculture such "committed relationships" can run months, sometimes weeks, even one night stands, but rarely years.

For New Agers, "spiritual partnerships" are only shades apart from domestic partnerships along the San Francisco "alternate lifestyle" model. But inevitably, such temporary unions are given a high sounding descriptive purpose—"higher good, soul evolution, etc." Zukav announces that "The archetype of spiritual partnership—partnership between equals for the purpose of spiritual growth—is emerging within our species."[31] It'll be interesting to ask the children of such transient unions how they feel about the merry go round of such spiritual partnerships.

Meanwhile, spiritual partnerships have another personal enhancement, empowerment. "The archetype of spiritual partnership reflects the conscious journey of multisensory humans to authentic power."[32] Note: you have just read a sentence that says nothing.

In this language of spiritual doublespeak, Zukav somehow moves to what he calls authentic power. And audiences are ready to hear about this is well. Everyone in America today wants to be empowered.

"Authentic Power"

New Age gurus occasionally offer the secrets to their brand of heightened awareness, usually in doublespeak. They offer a way to tap all this hidden potential. And Zukav draws the roadmap with the usual New Age doublespeak. "Conscious evolution through responsible choice is the accelerated way of evolution of the multisensory personality . . . Responsible choice is the conscious road to authentic empowerment."[33]

Real power is to create something with your own consciousness. It's something that God can do. When we do it, Zukav calls the process cocreation.

Of course many New Agers talk about co-creation, especially Barbara Marx Hubbard. As has been said before, co-creation is illustrated in lthe movie, *What Dreams May Come*, when Robbin Williams on the Deathplane constantly creates the textured psychedelic landscape of the realm around him, which, is simply a feedback mechanism for his level of consciousness. It is the essential methodology of the ancient Tibetan Buddhist text, the *Bardo Thodol*, where consciousness on the deathplane instantly determines the realm or Bardo the soul appears. The whole game is to sustain the Clear Light and hence merge with the godhead. I practiced cocreational consciousness exercises in India over twenty years ago when Zukav barely knew the term.

Of course I came to Christ because I eventually realized that even the euphoric experiences were demonic. It is the Great Lie, forever wrapping itself in new garb. And Postmodern New Agers wrap these age old concepts in new metaphors, but the ideas are the same.

The true *Seat of the Soul* is that it is desperately trapped and does not have the power to free itself. Only God can do that. And Grace is the only power in the universe that can transform a tainted soul into a pure where it can stand before an eternal, effulgent, transcendent, and holy God. The Holy Spirit showed me in South India that the my own soul was stained by sins that clung to it more tightly than the pull of the atoms out of which I am formed. Picture an ant glued to the ground by the wheel of a truck. It can't lift the tons of weight. The bootstrap method to perfection is a lie, a confidence game. Hence, *sola gratura*.

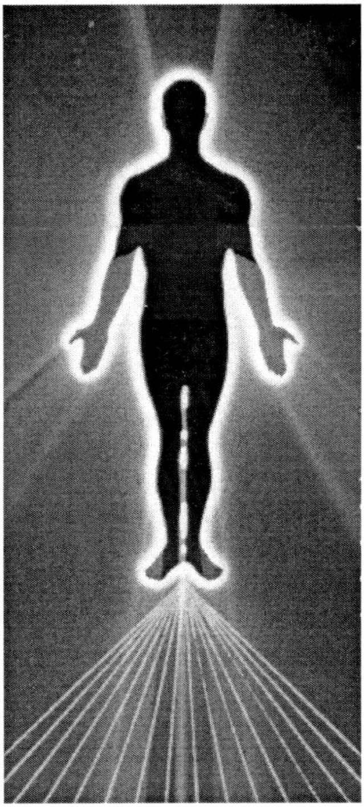

Zukav tells the public to trust the process and not worry. "Let Go. Trust. Create. Be who you are. The rest is up to your nonphysical Teachers and the Universe. Take your hands off the steering wheel. Be able to say to the Universe, 'Thy will be done,' and know it within your intentions."[34]

Years ago, when I was in India and the going got rough and I felt threatened that my whole mystical system was built on sand, an illusion in itself, I would sit back against a certain Banyan tree, inhale deeply in a sort of pranayam posture and say, exactly what Zukav now says, "Just trust the Universe." It was as though that would banish evil and any threat around me. But it was the spiritual equivalent of taking an opiate. It was like walking into a gang headquarters in East L.A., and saying, "I'll just trust them." Ignore danger and evil and it will just go away. Meanwhile, just ask someone who has been shot, raped, or torched if looking the other way will make it all go away.

Another horrible thing about today's New Age spiritual arena is that you can be deceived and feel absolutely great (in the short run and on the surface). That's why it's so dangerous. Years ago a fellow undergraduate confessed to me why he dabbled with heroin. I couldn't understand it because he had a brand new Astin Martin, a stunning girlfriend, and a terrific future in the family business. Then he confessed a dark secret, "The first time the spike went into my vein, I felt like God in heaven. I had entered paradise." I thought of the song by the Velvet Underground, *Heroin.* He never returned to paradise after the first few times on the needle, but devolved into the chaos of his own terrible addiction. The fact that he could feel so good, that very first moment in morphine paradise—-that sold him. It was as good as he had ever felt.

Thinking of him I recalled a Harlem Jazz artist of the Sixties named Lord Buckley who said (probably about heroin), "If you get to a place, and you can't get back—-then there you jolly well are, aren't you." It certainly described the feel of certain hellish LSD trips of my generation, things that some people had to ride out like a storm. I often thought of this quote from Lord Buckley in connection with the young college student playing with heroin. So it will be with many who have tried the *Soma* of New Age mind states. It will feel great for a while. Then the weight of it will become unbearable if they are fortunate enough to detect the weight gluing them down like the ant pinned to the ground by the wheel of a truck.

C.S. Lewis so aptly described the only thing in the universe powerful enough to remove this infinite mass of bondage through sin—- "The Weight of Glory." And so it is for those souls fortunate to see their true state, one of bondage and dire need of grace. That is the true human condition and not the self reincarnating towards godhood, as I once believed and as Zukav believes. Our generation has lost sight of grace and the weight of Glory. I would respond to Zukav, after my own dark night of the soul in India, "Don't trust the Universe. The only power in the Universe you can trust is Jesus Christ."

9

The Ancient Tradition—its Heart and Essence

Compared to accomplished yogis, the Western psychics are still aspirants, at times operating on a first-grade level. The accounts of India's most "evolved" yogis, such as Ramakrishna, Aurobindo, or Yogananda, reveal that their most elementary spiritual experiences begin where many of our Western psychics reach their limits, and they soon go far beyond them.

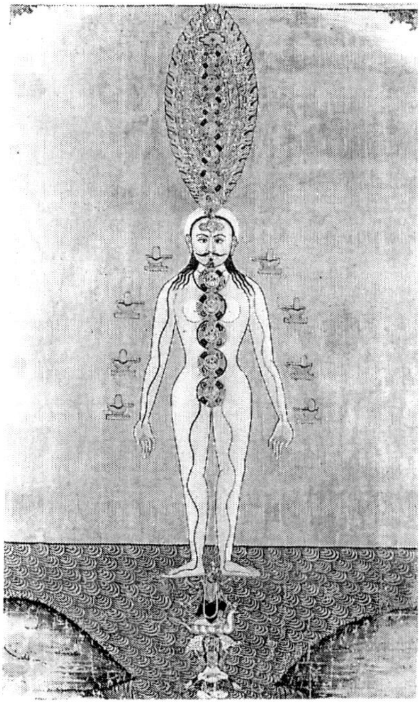

Yogis are linked directly with the ancient tradition, having systematized and perfected this tradition for centuries. Their astral travels end when they are spiritual teenagers, for they are shooting for the "big one" and are not interested in any small-time "food tasting in pastel planes," which "look just like earth." A yogi sneers at that kind of activity. He shoots "beyond the seven planes, and beyond the seven chakras, to what they all call *samadhi.*" *Samadhi* ("a state of deep concentration which results in union with ultimate reality") is the biggest death experience of all.

Let's not hide our eyes, for

America also has started to chase the "big one." In ten years, the counter-cultural daydream of a society unified around the experience of "the divine within" has become a concrete reality. It goes far beyond the fringe groups on which the media reports. Indeed, mystical doctrines have influenced wide areas such as science, commerce, politics, the arts, and psychology, as well as religion. The basic ideas about man, meaning, and God that are inherent in the ancient tradition are showing up as root premises in all sorts of contemporary trends.

This New Age occultism in America is a kind of "cosmic humanism." But it is tapped directly from the big conduit of the ancient tradition with its "hidden wisdom," so inherent to the Eastern path. This means that people at every level of today's culture are being conditioned to accept a definition of reality which ultimately denies the personal God of the Bible; asserts the autonomy, power, and inherent divinity of man; and condemns as obsolete any absolute statements of moral values.

C.S. Lewis offers insight into what is happening:

> Pantheism ['all-is-one'] is congenial to our minds not because it is the final stage in a slow process of enlightenment, but because it is almost as old as we are. It may even be the most primitive of all religions. It is immemorial in India. The Greeks rose above it only at their peak . . . their successors lapsed into the great pantheistic system of the Stoics. Modern Europe escaped it only while she remained predominantly Christian: with Giordano, Bruno, and Spinoza it returned. With Hegel it became almost the agreed philosophy of highly educated people . . . . So far from being the final religious refinement, pantheism is in fact the permanent natural bent of the human mind; the permanent ordinary level below which man sometimes sinks, but above which his own unaided efforts can never raise him for very long. It is the attitude into which the human mind automatically falls when left to itself. No wonder we find it congenial. If "religion" means simply what man says about God, and not what God does about man, then pantheism almost is religion. And religion in that sense has, in the long run, only one really formidable opponent-namely, Christianity."[1]

In the meantime, the spiritual anemia of the West has left this generation ravenous for reality, and therefore vulnerable to any "spiritual" novelty offered in the name of truth.

But let us look at the heart of the ancient tradition. The traditional systems of occult, mystical, and Eastern philosophy are patterned after the Great Lie of Genesis 3. Although intellectual constructions, they are intermingled, in the first instance, with a rare strain of reported experiences, the experiences of "cosmic totality." The *Upanishads* report that a drug known as "soma" was used to ignite some of the mystical experiences of the rishis. Likewise, someone sitting on a hill today eating peyote bulbs would typically give an experiential report that the stars, sky, trees, and all existence felt as though a unifying current of energy were holding it all together, and therefore *that* was the fundamental reality. The mystical systems that seek to interpret this experience can be analyzed into a number of related categories of thought. The four central presuppositions of this New Age Spirituality are:

1. *All is one*. Someone has a unitive experience. The effect is to dissolve all distinctions (the perceiver and the objects perceived) into a single, undifferentiated unity. This is where we obtain the first presupposition of monistic philosophy: there is only one reality in existence. From this, it follows that all apparent separations and oppositions (good and evil) are illusory manifestations of the single divine reality. All objects and individuals are merely parts of the all-inclusive one. The Hindus call it atma-paramatma, Brahman, and sat-chit-ananda ("being-consciousness bliss").

Nobel physicist Erwin Schrodinger said that his world view was derived from Vedanta and that ultimately there is only a single consciousness. "The external world and consciousness are one and the same thing, in so far as both are constituted by the same primitive elements."[2]

2. *Man is a divine being within.* If there is only a single reality in existence, then we are obviously parts or emanations of it. Our own "consciousness" provides the specific connecting link. In experiencing this reality, we experience our oneness with the "divine," as well as the essential divinity of our innermost nature. All forms of occult philosophy are united around the central belief that the inner or real self of man is God. This is the fundamental form of the primary lie spoken of in Genesis, "You will be like God" (Gen. 3:5, RSV).

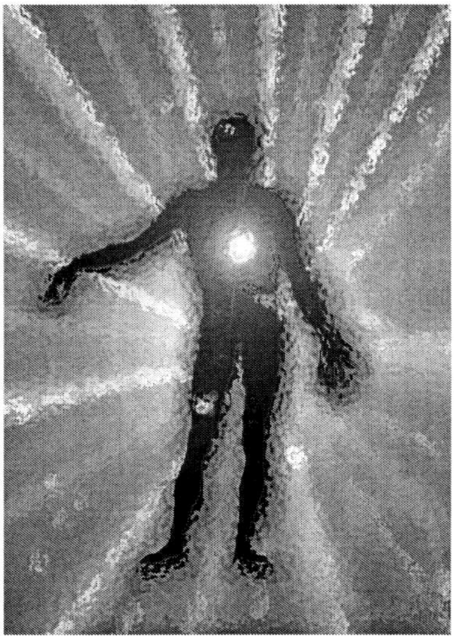

3. *Life's purpose is to realize the divine within.* No matter how the "divinity" of man may be defined by a particular path or sub tradition, the "way" is usually the path of supreme illumination or gnosis ("the attainment of supreme

knowledge"). Other mystical terms for it are *enlightenment*, *samadhi*, *at-one-ment*, *Nirvana*, *self-realization*, *satori*, and *God-consciousness*. This state of gnosis is usually reached by spiritual and psychic techniques, such as raja or kundalini yoga. Thus, the yogi finds union within the divine principle. The idea is that the person is a cosmic amnesiac who has forgotten his true divine identity, but the right system will remind him that he is really God after all. The closer he is to becoming God, the more conscious he becomes. The advanced yogi can supposedly remember back thousands of lifetimes which he has passed. He is seeking eternal death in order to extinguish himself from the painful round of rebirths, so death of his identity is required before he can wake up and become God. Thus, he is on a personal, subjective, and experiential trip and must discard any reliance which comes from the outside—faith, revelation, and information to the contrary.

4. *Self-realization leads to psycho-spiritual power*. This is where Uri Geller, Sai Baba, and Bubba Free John are, and where Wait Disney obtained his occult tales of "The Sorcerer's Apprentice." Things materialize and dematerialize, tables float, yogis levitate, and psychics see what is happening a hundred miles away.

As an initiate advances upon the path of gnosis, he becomes increasingly familiar with the divine "one" and its relationship to the phenomenal world of reality, "creation." Thus, he, as man-God, allegedly becomes master and creator of his own reality. Inasmuch as reality is supposedly composed of consciousness, the adept learns to control reality by controlling consciousness; matter is created or dematerialized with the facility of a divine conjurer.

It is here that mysticism merges into magic and vice versa. The palpable excuse for the magic miracle is pantheism, and the miracle might even be offered as proof that the consciousness of man can ascend to a level where it can control matter and events in a godlike manner. But the other way of interpreting this is that the man, not by an innate power, but by surrendering to an outside spiritual agency, is acting as a circuit through which the spirit power can manifest itself. Famed Israeli psychic and magician Uri Geller, on a BBC talk show, claimed that he received his power to bend nails by looking at them from a number of "cosmic intelligences" that channeled through him.

The fact remains that if any path, religion, or tradition includes even one of the four points mentioned above, it is certain that the thrust of its teaching runs counter to authentic Christianity. In the ancient tradition, man becomes God. In the Bible, that proposition is the ultimate lie. Man enters blissful communion with God through Christ alone, but he never becomes what he is not: God. Can a buffalo become a U.S. Congressman? Only if you believe in reincarnation. But nobody can prove it. Otherwise we would agree that the buffalo belongs in a field. India has tried placing the cow in positions of high office, and the results have been preposterous.

The main principles of the pantheistic system of man becoming God are: reincarnation, karma (the law that determines the level of birth), the belief that physical matter is maya (an illusion), and the methods of escape—yoga, meditation, idolatry, the mystery religions, the guru system, the techniques of astrology and tarot, special diets, drugs, and all manner of consciousness-expansion techniques to realize the "supreme identity."

But do these things help someone realize his godhood, or are they merely elaborate techniques for tenderizing him into finally swallowing whole that which a main part of him, his conscience, testifies against? Part of yoga's surgery is to kill the conscience, because a dead conscience makes becoming God much easier; there are no longer any squawks from the person's protesting conscience, which denies that he is God!

Where do all these paths lead? To death, the final exit—death of the ego, death of the personality, death of the will, death of all desires, death of the intellect, and ultimate death to living and to life. That is *moksha*. The ancient tradition says, "Die and you will be free." It has to work that way. If a person is not who he is, then his present personality has to be destroyed, because it is getting in the way of his finding out who he is.

The master prize of the yogis is *turya samadhi* ("supreme enlightenment"). Most of the religious writings of India's gurus speak about it. If it is reached, the yogi loses all desire to live; he does not eat or sleep, and after twenty-one days he dies. They say he is dead forever.

But let us leave "religion" for a second and look at the problem from man's viewpoint. Everybody has to deal with death, and there are only so many options one can select.

Just as death is final and total separation from the world we are so used to, so the awareness of that end shatters our attempt to find some sense or value to life in the here and now. A man sweating away on death row can hardly taste a lobster dinner if his mind is doing mental replays of the electric chair. Those who contemplate death while alive know that the show will be over sooner than they think; their house and property and friends will be taken away. If you feel uneasy when going away from your hometown with friends, then going alone to Chicago can unsettle you. But the trip to

Chicago is only for a tangible period, and you know exactly what you have to come back to. You may never come back from death, and you have nowhere to go. All the people and things on which you have leaned for so long will not go with you. Let's be honest. In some hidden recess of your mind, death is the ultimate terror. We don't know where we are going and we have no control of the process.

All "religion" in one sense is ultimately an attempt to come to terms with the pervasive and insidious fragmentation of our lives, which is introduced by the prospect of certain death. Man cannot escape a "religious" response to his condition, because individuals can never escape the fact that they must die. Specifically, this religious response is a groping for some ground of unity that will enable us to grasp an unknown harmony beyond the brittle disintegration of meaning which fractures all of our present hopes and pleasures.

But the available grounds for unity are strictly limited. Those who seek unification of broken reality must find it either in the living, personal, and transcendent God who speaks the cosmos into existence purposefully, or in some impersonal substrate of "being" which underlies the primordial duality of matter and energy.[3]

Thus, the religious desire for unity has two options for fulfillment: transcendence through Christ to contact with the eternal, holy God, or "subscendence" through mystical self-awareness to contact with the void.

To speak of God and his creation is to exhaust the scope of reality and existence. There is nothing else. Everything that exists is either God himself or is created by him. This leaves an open door for mystical religions and occult philosophies to take an extra step and say, "It's all God, and so am I." In effect, if you do not seek communion in the true transcendent God, you inevitably turn to some aspect of creation, the void, and call that God. After all, the Egyptians worshiped the sun, the Chaldeans the stars, and Hindus will enshrine almost anything. Since the creation itself is "fallen" (Rom. 8:19-23), the biblical conclusion is that mysticism declares the way by which one embraces the fulfillment of the curse of the fall here and now.

10

Dying in India—the Symptoms of the Ancient Tradition

Ravi Shankar's sitar concerts across the West combined with such books as Herman Hess's *Siddhartha* have done more for fascination with India than any campaign by the Indian tourist board. However, our more probing question is, ***If the Eastern system of metaphysics is really the highest and most sublime of truths on the face of the earth, what utopian evidences can we look for in India, the benefactor of this perennial spiritual wealth?*** ["By their fruits ye shall know them" (Matt. 7:20)].

If man really is God, as India and other Eastern cultures state, how does he fare in day-to-day living? Does he have dignity of life, or does his ignoble living reveal a soporific falsehood? Is true hope in the eyes of the dying, and do yogis communicate this when they die? Are the common people champions of this great spiritual heritage? If there is deceit, either willful or self-deceptive, the stench will eventually find a way to escape.

Certainly on the surface of things *Life*, *Atlantic Monthly*, *Newsweek*, *Time*, *U.S. News & World Report*, and *National Geographic* invariably report stories on India with abject horror regarding conditions there. For the past decades we have read of famine, floods, pestilences, disease, massive overcrowding, earthquakes, political corruption, and specific symptoms within the masses of people, which indicate why some of these conditions got out of hand. Natural conditions are inevitable, but many reporters also have tied attitudes and thought patterns to India's immense social problems: such things as caste, idolatry, ritual ignorance and superstition, stoical indifference, passivity, and ultimate resignation to the powers of fate.

One of the most brilliant films portraying the thousands of facets of India was made by a number of Frenchmen who smuggled their cameras into India and literally covered the land. Entitled *Phantom India*, it comprises eight parts of forty minutes each. Since the government of India and the Indians in general are hypersensitive about their national image, and since the movie is unflattering, the Frenchmen are now *persona non grata* in India and are not allowed to return. Journalists who apply for visas are usually grilled suspiciously.

All of us who have been in love with India have sought out redeeming places such as Himalayan waterfalls, Kashmiri lakes, Goan sea views, and tropical mango forests. But as I found when I visited those places with classic Indian vistas, they did not blot out the train rides to them—via Rishikesh, Calcutta, Hyderabad, Delhi, Bombay or Madras. Even while standing at some these beatific scenes, I always felt an underlying poverty and desolation that colored everything in sight.

The truth is, I went to India all primed for the land of romanticized images which I had envisioned. But what I saw appalled me. Was I prejudiced? To the contrary, I had pursued Eastern metaphysics, yoga, and Vedanta for much of a decade before going to India. After the swami at the Ramakrishna Mission in London spent two hours grilling me, he concluded that my wisdom and understanding of Advaita and Vedantic philosophy were far beyond my years, even for an orthodox Brahmin let alone a

Tal meditating in South India after over a year in India—and well over culture shock.

Westerner. Years later he read a book I wrote while in India after being a foremost disciple of India's highest-ranking miracle-working guru, Sathya Sai Baba, and declared it "flawless in advaitic doctrine" (I canceled the book, The *Amazing Advent*, on the day it was to come out.[1])

If the Hindu belief system which I followed was true, if anything, it should have prepared me for the culture shock I experienced, as should have the four and a half years which I had spent as a teenager in the Arab world. But 1 still suffered culture shock. Something was happening there that made me ask, "Are these people really right? Do they have the truth? Or are they the most lost and deluded people on earth?"After all, they were the ones who carried the legacy of the great Eastern tradition, whose culture was a laboratory, a vast social experiment, on what happens when you spend thousands of years en mass, living by what might be the highest mystical and spiritual principles on earth.

Then I heard of some of the Hindu customs such as suttee, in which the husband dies and his wife is thrown alive on the cremation fire along with his body and belongings. Then there is something which I call the fish-bait phenomenon. An eyewitness described it: "One of the gods in a village temple will tell the priest that it is time for another sacrifice, and the god tells him who the victim will be. So the village teams up, goes to the man's house with something like a huge fish pole, and baits his skin, running the entire length of his back, on something that resembles a massive fishhook. As he is dangling from a pole, they go trotting around the village with the fellow hanging in agony from the giant pole."

You can still see the scars today of the few who have survived this torture in order to appease some god. In the main, the British stamped out these two practices and others like them, but they still make one consider the origin of the ideas, as well as a system that can so readily absorb and justify them.

Even if the two above examples are disavowed by some Hindu sects, none can deny the idolatry, none can deny the yogic tortures, penances, pilgrimages, odd food habits, and other things which are found to be consistent with Hindu revelation and the self evolutionary concept of the East.

So the question remains: How is death approached by the masses, and how does the common man fare?

The answer is this: Indians live just to die. Death is the great release, and preparations are made for it from the moment of birth. Because of this, the land is full of machinations and rituals which anticipate and prepare for death. In that sense, it begins to resemble a spiritual Las Vegas, for death is the one big chance to pull the one-armed bandit on the wheel of rebirths and pop into the body of a king or a peasant the next time around. Of course Karma stands in the way of too much hope here. But there may be some yogic end runs.

One Tibetan idea is to go into death with the right frame of mind, for that will help determine where one goes. It is the same idea that some use to approach an LSD experience: one's preparation, or "set," determines what happens. A whole gamut of ideas exists on the best way to prepare; these ideas or techniques constitute the whole system of yoga, for they prepare one for ego death and physical death. *The Tibetan Book of the Dead* is a manual on different ways to enter death, while the Hindu mainstay, The *Bhagavad Gita*, enumerates various ways to die, all of which have become the great schools of yoga.

In *The Bhagavad Gita*, for example, one of yoga's main schools stemmed from a statement made by Krishna, the Pan-like blue black avatar of the Hindus, considered a divine embodiment of Vishnu (the preserver in the Hindu pantheon). Krishna looked at his disciple, Arjuna, telling him a method of liberation:

> Verily this divine illusion of mine [the universe], made up of the gunas [inert substance, active substance, and pure substance], is hard to surmount; but those who take refuge in me alone, they cross over this illusion."[2]

Krishna had previously told Arjuna that he (Krishna) is God, that he created the universe, and that only those who worship him can escape. The path of yoga that this created is known as *bhakti marga*, "the path of devotion." The aspirant literally consecrates his life to a given deity, building shrines to it, thinking of it constantly, and abiding in its name. That is the path through which the yogi seeks liberation.

Another statement made by Krishna is: "Whatever a man thinks of at the last moment when he leaves his body, that alone does he attain, 0 Kaunteya, being ever absorbed in the thought thereof."[3] From this ancient statement have come numerous yoga schools geared to controlling the mind, clearing it out, and preparing by "right thinking" for the inevitable death journey. *Vichara Atma* ("Who am I?"), the yoga of unending self-inquiry, utilizes this. *JJnana Yoga*, "the path of intelligent discrimination," also is partly based on this verse, as are such yogas as *Dhyana*, "mind-clearing concentration," and *Mantra Yoga*, the yoga of continually repeating the name of a given god until if death should catch one unawares, the name of that god is on the lips. This is one reason why some yogis are rapt in concentration, unmoving for hours and oblivious of the outside world.

Again Krishna tells Arjuna, "The omniscient, the ancient, the ruler, minuter than an atom, the supporter of all, of form inconceivable, effulgent like the sun, and beyond all darkness [the impersonal Brahman godhead, i.e., Krishna's true condition as he claimed]; he who meditates on this resplendent supreme Purusha, at the time of Death, with a steady mind, devotion and strength of yoga, well fixing the entire prana [life force] in the middle of the eyebrows, he reaches Him.'" The stakes are big here, for the promise is of the yogi reaching union with God. Later Krishna says that he becomes God because his *atma* ("true self") is one and the same as God.

Yoga is not really a means of appropriating grace. Rather, it is usually considered a high-powered method of short cutting the agonizingly long course of "evolution" which the soul takes before liberation. This is the jackpot referred to earlier. Even the *bhakti* marga path of devotion is contingent on the self-help method, because the aspirant still must work up the constant fury of adoration which is necessary to release him. In the end, it works out anyway, because only the aspirant who is so pure, so evolved (the result of millions of meritorious lifetimes), has the kind of *sathwic* ("pure") heart that puts him in this category. To reach the stage of being a proper *bhakta* ("Hindu religious devotee") takes millions of lifetimes. Certain gurus talk about grace, but the belief system of an impersonal monistic reality denies it.

The static eternal cannot give grace; it just is, and it is no more concerned about striving, suffering humanity than you or I lose sleep over the sight of rain washing ants off a tree trunk.

To accrue merit, millions of pilgrims swarm the humid ghats of Benares overlooking the Ganges River. The old, decrepit, infirm, and maimed will wait for the hour of death to plunge into the river, for they believe the river bathes the locks of Siva, the god of destruction, who supposedly sits at the base of the Himalayas. Some of their epics tell them all sorts of magical things about the Ganges River. The reality, though, is not romantic; it is sickening.

What the pilgrims are looking for is a cosmic loophole which will magically erase the endless accumulation of "karmic debt" they have built up

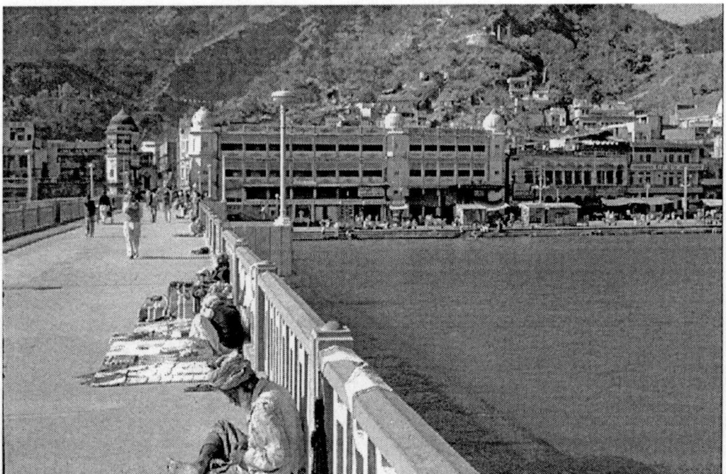

over myriad lives. These are the merciless records that form the balance sheet of every individual, spanning from his earliest appearance in the universe as a primitive geode to his present lifetime. These records totally ordain his fate.

The law of Karma ties a pilgrim to the agonies of birth after birth, saying he will not ever escape until he can lead a perfect life. Someone who has led a mediocre life, unable to rise above the paltriness of a rock breaker, has the grim prospect of coming back no higher than his present life. He believes he will be jammed back in the next birth into some crowded family of peasants. His fear is that an unaccounted sin, something he did as a child, will weigh him down on the death plane, forcing him to a far lower station in life than he expected. The out-and-out criminal has nothing to look forward to but a general dread of the unknown. He might be reborn as a mange-covered dog, and it may take millions of lives to work his way back from there to his present position. This is enough to make some people whimper in anguish, and they do.

Even the man of virtue has no easy prospect ahead. His pilgrimage road to immortality and perfection still winds ahead for an eternity, with perhaps millions of more lifetimes to go through. And just one little life of error, or one indulgence too many, will cast him back eons of time to some ignoble body. That is why the Hindu kisses the feet of the guru. Still, the long search for "grace" is something of a gamble, and the seeker does not really know the results of his life until he has died. Then maybe he can find out whether a propitiatory ceremony in some remote little temple sufficiently appeased the cosmic powers to elevate his fate. The Hindu theology of grace is complex and baffling (remember, grace cannot really exist).

What is the length of time that it takes a soul to end the hellish struggle for liberation? One of the most famous examples is from the lips of Krishna: as long as it takes a bird to utterly level the massive twenty-nine-thousand-foot slope of Mount Everest at the rate of one meager peck a year. Now think of being a coolie in Calcutta, or a tree snake—or who knows what else—for at least nine-tenths of that time. This prospect motivates people to do all kinds of extreme things. The formal term for this "day and night of Brahma" is *kalpa*. But even when one has finally entered the impersonal godhead, there is still the indubitable fact of the reoccurrence of the whole cycle of creation. It is eternal, going in and out of Brahman.

That great speedway of escape, yoga, can backfire too. The more high-powered it is, the more it can derail a person. The very ego that the initiate is trying to destroy can twist around and come back as a misshapen monster. Stories abound of yogis making large-scale goofs, reminiscent of the Dr. Jekyll and Mr. Hyde story, and loosing upon society some para-psychic freak who is misusing his powers. The Kriya yogis, Kundalini yogis, and Raja yogis traffic with such great spiritual powers that it is as if they are riding bareback on huge intercontinental missiles.

A Pictorial Glimpse

To sum it up pictorially, we can turn to Rishikesh, a Himalayan hill station, for a glimpse of where the yogic merit system leads. (I used to think of it as a spiritual Coney Island.)

Rishikesh sprawls along the Ganges, nestled between two rising hill slopes. The Ganges is still clear there, closer to its source of melting Himalayan glacial ice, hundreds of miles before it transforms into the opaque stench that washes the ghats of Benares. Yogic and monastic orders fan out from the cluttered town and polka-dot the hills and mountains on both sides of the sacred river. Typical of Indian holy spots, it swarms continually with pilgrims. The stench of incense, cow dung, urine, and garbage fills the air. Bazaars full of trinkets, gods, and holy items wind through the town between wooden tea stalls and vegetarian restaurants, which are glorified shacks always surrounded by mangy dogs. The dirty, fiery hot food is practically inedible. When I stayed there I could seldom sleep because of continual street pandemonium and the religious festivals which went on night after night for one of the thousands of gods; firecrackers exploded, and loudspeakers blared with speeches, bhajans ("songs"), and dramas.

Outside of Rishikesh, pilgrims drift along the road with sacred cows, going from one temple to another. They range from the austere Shaivite sadhus wearing loincloths and saffron shawls, covered with ash, their knotted hair caked with cow dung, to ordinary citizens. Street gurus and pundits ("wise or learned men") give discourses to collections of passersby and beggars, who line up on

the street with their begging bowls in front of them. Not too far off are the leper colonies.

Farther away are the hidden and fortressed ashrams ["secluded dwellings or retreats"), ranging from the Sivananda divine-life ashram to the newly built "Shankaracharya Nagar," Maharishi's academy of meditation, which is surrounded by a barbed wire fence, and where its non hippy Western entrants are checked like CIA employees. It has auditoriums, lecture halls, dormitories, wooden cabins, and closed-circuit TV. It also has the highest initiation fee in town.

But at the base of the verdant mountain, across the river from Rishikesh, perhaps serving as a statement of the ancient origins of transcendental meditation and all the other schools of yoga, wind labyrinthine shrines, holy gardens, and temples housing gaudy and strange idols. To fully communicate the effect, here is my initial reaction, recorded in ***Avatar of Night:***

> The temples interconnected with weird gates, entrances, and hallways were painted in ghastly bright pastels that highlighted their otherworldly shapes. The most unhinging section of all was a temple with a courtyard of huge cement lotuses and figures that portrayed scenes out of the Hindu epics. Above the main pathway to the entrance, elevated glass cases protruded from the walls which contained life sized manikins of the main Hindu gods, clothed, four-armed, blue-black, with enigmatic death-mask expressions that either stared far off or right down at you through either two or four perfect glass eyes.

> On every trek to the ashram they confronted me from their elevated dusty cases, and I inevitably wondered what state of mind a man would have to be in to see them as divine. Certainly the smell of cotton candy, salt-water taffy, combined with the sickly burblings of a Wurlitzer organ would end my ambivalence. But for now, there was always the possibility that I was hung up by "cultural variables." Their system would say

> that for every man there is a unique way of approaching the absolute. Yet why did these temples not generate a feeling of exuberance or sanctity, but rather of voidness, desolation, and death? And if this feeling was a sample of what the rishis called *Nirvana*, and should *Nirvana* be an absolute increase of this force, then perhaps it was the most terrible cosmic insanity conceivable.[5]

The effect of those sights is like that of a giant hundred-foot cement ice-cream cone, spray painted metallic purple and green, serving as a lure of the great worlds to meet the pilgrim after death.

Those who are on the road to paradise fight their fates like dung beetles forever rolling balls. Every aspirant is a thin and weather beaten island unto himself. All forms of austerity and discipline are witnessed, from the quiet ascetic sitting motionless for years, fed by passersby, to the desperate groans and chants of sadhus repeating a single *mantra* ("holy word") again and again all day, day in and day out. Occasionally one sees the path of true mortification: sun gazers who are blind from looking at the sun over the years, or those whose arms are still raised, wispy and atrophied, due to their constantly holding them up in some freeze position. Always there are the wandering ash-covered Shaivite sadhus ("renunciants, followers of Siva' ') carrying a trident, wearing radhraksha beads, frequently sitting on a little mat under a sun umbrella, and often smoking ganga ("hashish").

Then there are the peculiar tapas ("purifying disciplines") of each ashramic ("monastic' ') order, with each guru teaching a devoted band of followers his own brand of enlightenment: odd diets, yogic postures, power breathing (pranayama), chanting for eighteen hours at a stretch to the accompaniment of cymbals and drums, fasting, going without sleep, bowing and posturing to shrines and particular deities, and all manner of physical hardship and denial. As one might expect, there is really not a great deal of exuberance and joy around the town of Rishikesh, no matter what anybody says.

In Lhasa and Kathmandu, neighboring India's borders, untold numbers of people can be found madly spinning what might look like toys, but what are actually Buddhist prayer wheels. They save the people from having to utter a mantra for each spin, and do the work for them. Some people look quite frenetic as they spin away, obviously intent on chalking up a great deal of merit. Prayer wheels differ in size, rotation-speed, and numbers of mantras within them. A few of the people in the merchant class are the real "pinball wizards," for they have electric fans with huge blades upon which are written thousands of names of gods. At so many RPMs per hour, the totals on the mantric scoreboard are uncountable. I will avoid the obvious detailed progression, merely mentioning the great potential of vast electromagnetic centrifuges containing billions of names of a god by the use of microphotography. *The Tibetan Book of the Dead* teaches essentially the same thing as Krishna said about repeating the name of a god at the point of death.

Solomon and the ancient prophets of Israel, in speaking of pagan ritual and idolatry, dismissed them as terminal futility and blasphemy. The pagans who did such things were portrayed as making monkeys of themselves. Paul the apostle claimed that such people were in bondage to demons.

Finally, what would make so many intelligent people stoop to such acts? A most sophisticated, subtle, and palpable lie. The very concepts of mystical philosophy were certainly potent enough in my life to cause me to do any number of things. It takes a most thoroughly seduced intelligent man to bow before a stone image, while a peasant will do it without a moment's thought. That is why most of India at one time or another bows before some formidable stone god. This is the hundred-foot cement ice-cream cone! The Bible declares it, the philosophy, the idols, and the acts to be ***abominations.*** Who wants to go into death deceived?

Where did it all start? Who first had the idea that death is the ultimate release and that to prepare for it one must perform a lot of mumbo jumbo? We are coming to that.

11

Death in Babylon

For those who seek to understand it, death is a highly creative force. The highest spiritual values of life can originate from the thoughts and study *of death . . . . It's* not *just a question of* good *and evil, heaven* or *hell, as you will* see *when* you *read the selection* on *Hinduism and Buddhism.*

In the decades to come *we may* see one *universe,* one *humankind,* one *religion that unites* us *all in a peaceful world.*[1]—Elizabeth Kubler-Ross

Having just looked at the giant sprawling amoeba of Eastern mysticism gathering everything but true Christianity into itself, we now need to understand why the Bible predicts that as history winds down some giant syncretistic religion with a mystical core known as "Mystery Babylon" will be the reigning religion of the world. The Book of Revelation in the Bible emphatically speaks of a one-world religion and refers to it as "an abomination." Under its banner will be the diverse occult practices justified by the divine within concept, those same arts practiced by Babylon of old. It will be a mystery religion, awesome in its subtlety. Yet the living God of the Bible shall declare war upon it and consume it in judgment.

The "mystery of iniquity," according to Paul the apostle, is the dynamic of why one man would embrace the final unitive counterfeit religion and why another man would shun it. People are accountable deep within themselves, and God alone shall completely reveal the secret of choice, says the Bible.

It seems that if we have a genuine love of the truth, no matter where we are, God will guide us into the truth. He will provide a way. There have been conversions deep in the heart of India, indeed Borneo, that bare this out.

If we are to understand that Mystery Babylon is to become a world system (as the Bible predicts, replacing Christianity), it is important to know two things. We must appreciate what the Babylon of old embodied, and we must be able to pick out the present building blocks that will form the coming world religion's system of Mystery Babylon. It is my contention that one of these building blocks is the doctrine on death arising out of the "breakthroughs" by thanatologists such as Moody and Kubler-Ross. Since the Kubler-Ross plan of afterlife is pantheistic, the stage is set for further progress toward the unitive system, for death can be another hub around which all the world religions can be forced to merge.

Let us examine Babylon of old. One of the greatest historical records is found in the Bible, which says that Babylon sinned; it missed the mark. The Hebrew word for "sin," chatha, means "go wide of the mark." In its essence, sin is a constant preference for the desires, assertions or intuitions of one's self over the proclamations of God. In Babylon's case, its root sin was its "secret knowledge," which God abhorred.

Brooks Alexander reports:

> The precise nature of this secret knowledge is indicated by the mention of Babylon. In the Old Testament, Babylon was the persistent enemy of God and of God's people, both spiritually and politically. The city personified the continuous pressure of false religion against the redemptive designs of God. In chapter 47 of Isaiah we see God's scathing condemnation of Babylon's spiritual corruption.
>
> The context is especially important. We should notice that the preceding four chapters are placed as a deliberate contrast to the unveiling of the Babylonian error. Through Isaiah, God makes an overpowering revelation about himself. The keynote of this tremendous self-disclosure is the phrase, "I AM." The pivotal assertion, "I AM THE LORD . . . " is in fact repeated 21 times in Isaiah 42.

The climax of God's self-description is reached in Isaiah 45:18—"I am the Lord, and there is no other . . . I did not say to the offspring of Jacob, 'Seek me in chaos' [or "the void' ']. I the Lord speak the truth, I declare what is right."

From the peak of that pure, clear divine statement, it is a downhill slide to chapter 47. There God evaluates the spiritual realities behind the facade of the Babylonian religion. He strips bare the shameful deceit of her "wisdom."—"Now therefore hear this, you lover of pleasures, who sit securely, who say in your heart, 'I am, and there is no one besides me' . . . [judgment] . . . shall come to you in a moment . . . shall come upon you in full measure, in spite of your many sorceries and the great power of your enchantments. You felt secure in your wickedness, you said, 'No one sees me'; your wisdom and your knowledge led you astray, and you said in your heart, 'I am, and there is no one besides me'" (Isaiah 47:8-10).

The meaning of this could not be clearer. Babylon was condemned because its religion was based upon an illegitimate usurpation of divinity, an idolatrous identification of the human self with God.

> We should not mistakenly assume that this unsparing denunciation is directed merely against the self-glorification of man's limited ego, the 'social self' or 'biographical identity' of the individual. A much more radical presumption is in view here. Secular history confirms for us that the distinguishing mark of the Babylonians was their cosmic view of man's nature. Historically speaking, the entire Chaldean culture, Babylon included, is known to have been deeply rooted in the esoteric science of astrology. Every aspect of this ancient civilization, its rule as well as its ritual, was charged with the power of its occult symbology and the secret wisdom of its priestly initiates.
>
> The most significant religious edifice in Babylon was the Ziggurat, which in addition to serving as an astrological observatory was an astral temple symbolically representing the structure of reality. The Ziggurat as the "cosmic mountain" tied together heaven and earth. It was the all-inclusive image of the totality of the universe. In the ritual act of ascending the altar (and edifice), the priests acted out the stages of 'god-realization,' and the inner meaning of man's oneness with the cosmos. The Babylonian monarch himself was the focus of the occult power channeled through the activities of the priesthood. He was regarded as a divine being, a god-man. And it was he who contained and maintained the cosmic order on behalf of those he ruled. The monarch's distinctive royal function was to integrate in his own being the powers that govern the universe and his society.
>
> In all respects the esoteric core of the Babylonian gnosis was substantially identical to what we now encounter through Eastern and occult mysticism. The chief distinction is that in those days it was more strictly distributed. In our own times, the seal of secrecy has been broken, and "Mystery Babylon" is spread abroad.
>
> In the highest moment of serene ecstasy the initiate, properly speaking, does not find God. Rather, the mystery of his own being supremely asserts itself. At the end, the only thing that appears to exist (in his universe) is the human self-consciousness moving in sovereign solitude over the void abyss of void existence.
>
> This occult illumination is precisely the opposite of a God-centered orientation to reality. It is radically man-centered and thus it becomes the perfected expression of the Great Lie ("you will be as God") through the logical necessity of its own false presuppositions.[2]

Brooks and I agree that the Bible shows that knowledge, power, and wisdom exist in this other spiritual system, but the system is not according to God. It is based on the lie of the "divine within," and it gets its power from another source. Ezekiel, as God's mouthpiece, points to Babylon and says,

"Your heart is proud, and you have said, 'I am a god, I sit in the seat of the gods . . . ' yet you are but a man, and no god" (Ezek. 28:2, RSV).

When Cyrus the Mede crushed Babylon, its secret religion did not disappear from the face of the earth; rather, the whole body of beliefs moved in a variety of directions. Its gods, bearing slightly different names, but in their identity remaining the same, moved to other cultures. Not only did the gods migrate, but across the centuries the very depth of the mystery religion continued to expand. Far from being extinguished, it grew in the very botanical tank of India, where the full genius of the deception would come into bloom, only to blow the spores back across to the Western world. But Babylon of old had the antitypes of the original avatars, celestial beings, mediums, meditators, astrologers, and psychics from whence originated the doctrine of reincarnation in India today. Nimrod, the founder of Babylon, claimed that he would reincarnate as the avatar Tammuz.

Ancient gods

Babylonian gods and goddesses migrated to India, not merely as the idols of the gods, but their cosmic personalities. These beings, one can imply from the statements of the Apostle Paul, come from the celestial hierarchies of demonic hosts. They are not cultural interest items, or simply Jungian archetypes in the collective unconscious of man, but, in fact, ancient spirit personalities who have tried to mold history across the ages. In the Indian culture, they have been identified more than once as beings of light.

> The Babylonians, in their popular religion, supremely worshiped a goddess mother and son [Semiramis and Tammuz]. From Babylon, this worship of the mother and child spread to the ends of the earth. In Egypt, the mother and child were worshiped under the names of Isis and Osiris. In India, even *to this day*, as Isi and Ishwara . . . .
>
> In Babylon, the title of the goddess-mother as the "dwelling place of God," was Sacca, or in the emphatic form, Sacta, that is, "the tabernacle." Hence, *at this day*, the great goddess in India, wielding all the power of the god whom she represents, is called "Shakti" or "the tabernacle." [Shakti, as is commonly known, is the female counterpart of the great god Siva.]
>
> It was an essential principle of the Babylonian system, that the sun or Baal was the one only god. When, therefore, Tammuz was worshiped as God incarnate, that implied also that he was an incarnation of the Sun. In the *Hindu mythology, which is admitted to* be essentially Babylonian, this comes out very distinctly. There, Surya, or sun, is represented as being incarnate, and born for the purpose of subduing the enemies of the

gods, who, without such a birth, could not have been subdued. [There is equally as conclusive evidence regarding the origins of Krishna, Rama, Vishnu, Brahma, Matraiya's Dagon, and a host of other gods and goddesses.[3]

To the pilgrims who swarmed Rishikesh, these gods and goddesses are celestial beings commuting forever from death planes and paradise worlds to the earth. They are cosmic personalities, known to mediumistically possess their worshippers. One of the highest boons of the *sankirtan* ("chanting and singing the names of gods and goddesses for extremely long periods") is that the deity begins to manifest itself through the devotees. Even the great yogis report this phenomenon during the course of their spiritual growth. Ramakrishna was observed by his devotees becoming possessed by Lakshmi, Kali, and Vishnu at various times.

On the higher levels of Hindu *advaitist* ("monistic, or nondualist") philosophy, the kernel of the mystery religion unfolds progressively as the significance of the gods and goddesses is explained.

The god or goddess now becomes a cosmic essence or quality, a handle in the realm of maya which the mystic can use to vault into the godhead, the non dual impersonal ocean of Brahman. In short, it is the secret doorway enabling temporal man to become God. Thus, through the eyes of the advanced mystic, the gods and goddesses of the pantheon represent personalizations of abstract higher reality; yet they supposedly have consciousness and can embody persons. Allegedly, they appear before the aspirant for the sake of taking him to the void. Then the gods and goddesses, like the realized mystic, merge back into the indissoluble ocean of Brahman, from whence they never really left but only appeared to leave.

The gods and goddesses become the chrysalis through which the mystic passes in becoming deity. In the case of Ramakrishna, he adored Kali. As a mere human ego, at one point he considered it blasphemy to identify himself as one with Kali. But in time the goddess took him over so much that he found full identification with her. At that point the guru of Ramakrishna told him to shatter her asunder by breaking her image in himself on a shard of glass. He did, and so he was no longer Kali. Instead, he supposedly became "the eternal one," reaching *samadhi* or enlightenment in the process. He went from the dual plane of our ephemeral universe, with its gods

and goddesses, to the unborn, "one without a second." Ramakrishna is the prototype success story in our presently emerging mystery religion.

Now we begin to understand that in the mystery religion the gods and goddesses are only intermediates between man and the ultimate God-self. They stand at the gates of death—ego death, physical death, and death to our universe—and beckon the worshiper and mystic through. It is precisely this function that we see among the gods and goddesses and cosmic beings in *The Tibetan Book of the Dead*, so highly praised by Moody. They are the beings of light. The same beings of light fill the accounts of yogis in India and Roshis in Tibet, as we see in our modern accounts. It is a one-for-one correspondence. A being of light is a being of light. If a yogi (as opposed to an American in a hospital) experiences one, and experience is our measuring rod, do we dare deny that there is any difference?

The most famous Indian *Siddha* yogi ["one who has attained perfection in occult powers") in recent history, Muktananda, had an experience with a being of light just before he became "enlightened:"

> As I again sat for meditation, I felt there was a great commotion around. My entire body started aching and automatically assumed *padmasana*, the lotus posture . . . I felt severe pain in the knot [manipur chakra] below the navel. I tried to shout but could not even articulate . . . . Next I saw ugly and dreadful demon-like figures. I thought them to be evil spirits.
>
> I then saw blazes of fire on all sides and felt that I too was burning. After a while I felt a little better. Suddenly I saw a *large ball of light* approaching me from the front; as it approached, its light grew brighter and brighter. It then entered unobstructed through the closed doors of my *kutir* ["hut"] and merged into my head. My eyes were forcibly closed and I felt a fainting sensation. I was terrified by the powerfully dazzling light.[4]

What we see between the Babylonian gods and goddesses, the Indian gods and goddesses, the modern American reports of premortem beings of light, and the encounters with beings of light by Indian yogis is that they are all of the same lineage. This is a key building block, supplied by the scientific method, that forms the graft to wed the mystical system of Babylon and the mystical system of India with the increasing trend of cosmic humanism on the world scene.

Not only does Moody's being of light tie in with the Eastern system, but so does Kubler-Ross's view of who man really is, his true self. In the concluding chapter of her book *Death: The Final Stage of Growth*, her beliefs emerge. Kubler-Ross chose to entitle the chapter "Omega," the well-known symbol for eternity in the Bible. Christ says, "I am the Alpha and the Omega," three times in the Book of Revelation. I will quote Kubler-Ross liberally to solidify what I hope has become an obvious point. Ask yourself whether this is the biblical definition or the Eastern mystical definition of who man really is.

> There is no need to be afraid of death . . . death is the key to the door of life . . . . It is essential that you become aware of the light, power, and strength within each of you, and that you learn to use those inner resources in the service of your own and others' growth . . . . Through commitment to *personal growth* individual human beings will also make their contributions to the growth and development—the evolution-of the whole species to become all that humankind can and is meant to be. *Death is the key to that evolution* . . . . *The answer is within you.* You can become a *channel* and a source of great inner strength. But you must
>
> give up everything in order to gain everything . . . . When human beings 'find a place of stillness and quiet at the highest level of which they are capable, then *the heavenly influences can* pour *into them*, re-create them, and use *them* for the *Salvation* of mankind.' [Kubler-Ross quotes *The Quiet Mind*] . . .
>
> There is no total death. Only the body dies. The *Self* or spirit, or whatever you wish to label it, is eternal. You may interpret this in any way that makes you feel comfortable . . . . You may be more comfortable and comforted by a faith that there is a source of goodness, light, and strength greater than any of us individually, yet still *within* us *all*, and that each *essential self* has an existence that *transcends* the finiteness of the physical and *contributes to that* greater power . . . . Death, in this context, may be viewed as the curtain between the existence that we are conscious of and the one that is hidden from us until we raise that curtain . . . . It is our purpose as human beings to grow—to *look within* ourselves to find and build upon that source of peace and understanding and strength which is our inner selves, and to reach out to others with love, acceptance, patient guidance, and hope for what we all may become

together."[5]

The message is clear: the true self transcends death because within it is the source of transcendent existence. The seeds of perfection are within; salvation is from within. The self is eternal and self-sufficient, and within the self is the key, the guide, and the answer for self-evolution. This is the identical definition that Vedantins, yogis, and' other forms of Hindus use for "the true self" or *atma.* The Hindu teaching is that the "Atma evolves to Paramatma," which means "the self becomes God." It is a far cry from the biblical account of a fallen and bankrupt soul, incapable of saving itself, whose only salvation is in Christ. Christ told the people that they did not have it within themselves to save themselves.

Indeed, these words of Kubler-Ross could be direct quotes from any number of famous mystics and yogis; the same phrases can be lifted from the writings of Aurobindo, Ramakrishna, Yogananda, Meher Baba, Madam Blavatsky, or Sat Prem. One wonders what her source of inspiration really was.

As mentioned earlier, Kubler-Ross has a spirit guide, Salem, which by biblical standards makes her a medium.

Consider the following description of Kubler-Ross, and forget the sweet reassurance of her words:

> Then, visibly moved and emanating a glow of awe and wonder, she [Kubler-Ross] shared with us a profound mystical experience that had happened to her only the night before in the midst of a group of seventy-five people. She prefaced her narrative with the remark that only a short time ago she would not have found it possible to speak these words at a public forum. "Last night I was visited by Salem, my spirit guide, and two of his companions, Anka and Willie. They were with us until three o'clock in the morning. We talked, laughed and sang together. They spoke and touched me with the most incredible love and tenderness imaginable. This was the highlight of my life."[6]

If we are honest with ourselves about wanting to know the truth, and the Bible speaks about this matter of familiar spirits and spirit guides, we are blinded and liars if we do not consider what it says. It does not compromise.

> And when they say to you, "Consult the mediums and the wizards who whisper and mutter," should not a people consult their God? Should they consult the dead on behalf of the living? (Isa. 8:19, NASB).

We find that at the time of the Babylonian mystery religion, the occult threat of the depraved practices of the Canaanites was so great, its intermixing with God's truth so abhorrent, that God warned about it severely:

> Do not turn to mediums and wizards; do not seek them out, to be defiled by them: I am the Lord your God (Lev. 19:31, RSV).
>
> If a person turns to mediums and wizards, playing the harlot after them, I will set my face against that person, and will cut him off from among his people (Lev. 20:6, RSV).
>
> A man or a woman who is a medium or wizard shall be put to death; they shall be stoned with stones, their blood shall be upon them (Lev. 20:27, RSV).

The Bible leaves us with no neutral category in which to put Kubler-Ross. Being a medium is not an "OK thing." You may say it is harmless, but how do you really know? How many millions of years, tangibly, have you existed in full consciousness without interruption to make a judgment on your own authority? This excludes reincarnation. If you said, "ten million years," I would have to say that those years are a fleeting second compared to the eternity of God, and he says an unequivocal no to fooling with familiar spirits.

At the heart of the occult doctrine is the divine-within concept, which was at the center of Babylon's mystery religion, with its concomitant occult arts. This mystery religion did not disappear when Babylon was destroyed, but instead continued to grow in India and other regions of the East. What we find today is a rapid acceptance of mystical precepts in the Western world. Indeed, this new mysticism promises to unify the human race into a world brotherhood, but at a price. Its implied reward is the bestowal of godhood on man. Consistent with ancient Egypt, Babylon, India, and the mystics of all ages, it views death as no more than a stage, a transition, for no other reason than that if the soul is immortal, as the higher self, then death is ultimately an illusion. Death becomes mankind's greatest friend. So we have come full circle to the seductive promise of godhood in the Garden of Eden.

Meanwhile, in the West, how did we get from reason to mysticism? Are we starting to see the eclipsing of modernism and its smug bias that states flatly that there is no supernatural?

12

A Perplexed West

The power of the written word affects history in remarkable ways. Visualize a man scrawling on a pad of paper in a candle-lit room in some shabby, ignominious part of town in the mid-1800s. He is a man we would pass on the streets of London among the throngs of urchins and ordinary folk and think no great thing of it; we would not look twice. In the silence of his study--should we come zooming in by some timeless TV camera--we would hear the scratching of his pen, and we would see the writ unfolding. Should that writ blow away or fall in some trash can, we would feel that the course of the world, the immense gears of history, could proceed well without it. It would make no difference.

Little would we realize that the writ would telescope across half a century to begin an event as titanic as any in modern history. It would create a power bloc encompassing almost half the earth, including the Soviet Union, that sprawling land mass with its Red armies, sophisticated weaponry, and 300 million citizens in ideological enslavement. Russia would churn the world like a mighty dragon about to snap its chains and engulf the world. Yet the power of the writ would extend farther to another land mass, Red China, and add another billion people to the sum.

The writ was *The Communist Manifesto*. The man was Karl Marx, who had left Germany and moved to London. To this day that potent writ continues to shake the world's events, which shows how one body of ideas can affect the course of history. In fact, it has been ideas all along, behind the events of history, which have dethroned one age and thrust up another, including all of the Western world. Far from being an innocuous ivory-tower pastime, ideas have changed civilizations in the most concrete ways. Karl Marx borrowed from Hegel and Feuerback, and so on, back through history. Most citizens of a specific age cannot articulate the spirit of that age, but it stirs in their thoughts and within them.

The thoughts written on a philosopher's table in one century can rule another century. Marx's socialism continues to proliferate under new configurations. It is the creed of the all-powerful State. Socialistic directives are being enacted to this day, slowly changing the face of America as with other Western nations now that it is called "socialism."

From what philosopher's tables has our culture come? We ask this in the full light of Christianity's fate. We have chosen to believe the supreme wisdom of the philosopher's stone, for the revelation of man has usurped the revelation of God in the West.

What is our present mood regarding the meaning of existence? How does this affect our view of death?

The reigning view among the educated, which has held sway in the West for a very long time, says there is no afterlife in a godless universe based on pure random accident. This view has been most recently repackaged in "*the blind watchmaker*" image coming from the biological sciences with Richard Dawkins, whose book bears the same title, leading the pack. If life has no ultimate meaning, obviously death has no significance. The seeds of this view go all the way back to the German rationalists and the British empiricists who began. to throw God out of the equation centuries ago. From Darwin to Bertrand Russell, Freud, to Carl Sagan and Richard Dawkins, a long line of Western academics and intellectuals have added to the picture. It is a picture of hopelessness. Live today for tomorrow you die.

The present scientific view of the universe leaves no room for meaning or for love. Love is an inexplicable oddity, almost an embarrassment. Man is told that love may well be a luxury that he can no longer count on, for present belief leaves a diminishing place for it. The deep assurance of the soul, which Christianity provided when its world view reigned, has been erased. Now only questions and speculations remain, and many of the speculations are hopeless.

Farther down the intellectual food chain, campus moods continue to be either grim or hedonistic. The cynical aside has become the common currency of the day, while few public figures draw genuine respect. Sex roles are turning upside down, and marriage as an institution is on the brink of collapse. People are suspicious of one another and wonder who, if any, is truly good and trustworthy. Is goodness possible? it is asked. Everyone seems to be "in it for himself."

In the scientific community the idea of finding meaning to life has all but been abandoned as a romantic and antiquated notion that suited a bygone era.

Scores of scientific authorities—as oracles who have supplanted God—openly contradict one another as they offer solutions to the world's problems. Meanwhile, the landscape of civilization groans like a giant beast. The skyline is ugly, for in place of the natural wilderness that was once America, raw pollution oozes out as the fecal matter of sprawling civilization. Environmentalists examine air and water and proclaim the ecological crisis. Everything that man touches seems to turn to sludge.

But death is also a threat in an atmosphere of negativity. We either shut it out of our minds and cellophane wrap our coffins, or we dispose of death with nervous quips of black humor. Our lives go at such a furious pace that we do not allow the thought of death to creep in, while solitude is avoided at all costs, in the event that we might become morbid. Then come all the escapes: liquor, TV, sex, drugs, hobbies, work, sports, and anything else that will get in the way and shut out the growing vacuum. Yet many of the escapes are no longer working, now that it is possible to be lonely even in a crowd of friends. Man seems to be reaching a dead end, the self-fulfilling prophecy of Existentialist Jean Paul Sartre's *No Exit*.

As a child of our age, I was only too familiar with the contemporary malaise. Cynicism was epidemic at every school I attended. To echo Bob Dylan's words, it seemed that "not much was really very sacred." The ideals so exalted in the "old days" were gutted with the glibness of TV talk shows, as we questioned if there was any enduring value to love, marriage, life, God, or anything else. To be sure, we were not oblivious to the fact that such things were crumbling about us in a stock market crash of values that plummeted as doubts increased. "What is worth living for?" we asked. This was the dilemma that caused so many of us to act in rage. We were a generation that protested in disillusionment, rioted, marched, jibed, and got into trouble constantly.

But on a deeper level, such acts were simply the ghosts of the previous generations' beliefs about life coming back to haunt them in full-blooded imagery. The youth provided the embarrassing afterthoughts. After all, how can death be a sacred institution in an age of relativism? Who or what deserves respect in a universe with man at the top? There are no ideals. Nor is there freedom or dignity in a Skinnerian behavioristic world.

Jean Paul Sartre

We were reacting with a gut response to a post-Christian world. The experts clearly gave us the message that there was no personal God, only the hope of man saving himself. And it was not altogether clear, either, who man was.

A contemporary cartoon summed it all up by picturing a child standing before a group while "decked out" in flippers, ballet dress, football helmet, catcher's mask, Donald Duck beak, hockey kneepads, with a baseball bat in one hand and a baton in the other. Identity confusion was the order of the day.

Desmond Morris told us man was a "naked ape." Monod, a geneticist, told us man was an accident, and the Existentialists such as Camus and Sartre told us man had no meaning or significance, that life was just a joke. Scores of Sartre's university students at the Paris Sorbonne wound up jumping into the Seine River to end their lives.

The philosophy of science left us with such a bleak picture of existence that there was only one other option (if one was no longer willing to consider revealed religion): ***mysticism***. That door was hurled open with almost violent force. Many threw out the god of cold logic with utter disdain and jumped into the "higher gear" of non rational intuition. Postmodernism was eclipsing the Modernism that had reigned for 200 years—and it all happened in the 60s. In the wave of the Beatles, Timothy Leary, psychedelia, the occult, and the Eastern gurus, Haight-Ashbury and beyond sang about flower power, and a new generation of mystically oriented youth was on the way.

Scientists from the 60s would try to make the facts of science fit a new paradigm and harmonize with the view that everything is evolving into pure

consciousness. Carl Sagan smiles on the cover of *Newsweek*, assuring us that we are not alone in the universe (there's probably no God but there are aliens!—as the film ***Contact*** assures us). Books like *The Tao of Physics* proliferate, while anthropologist Castaneda tells us of his mystical findings through the revelations of shamans on the desert.

Ergo, the bridge for the new view of death was laid—it is both post-Christian yet spiritual. And indeed, death research would close the gap between present knowledge and the mystical view of afterlife. The new faith of death would then triumphantly demolish the bankruptcy of despair coming from the rationalism of the modern age. Even the exaltation of reason might be discarded in the scramble. This is how Moody and Kubler-Ross found such a timely niche in the historical progression of our age.

The long tyranny of humanist despair could now be exchanged for a groundless hope when the gentle doorway of death eases into a blissful love-filled hereafter. What a balm to replace a cruel and impersonal world.

Yet biblically, this is the sweetest lie of all. God, having been removed by modernism, is then replaced by another spiritual system—one that has been around before. This too is part of a sobering pattern.

13

The Death of God

How was God disposed of in a way that was able to bring in this new view of the supernatural?

The hat-trick went something like this. The naturalistic view moved swiftly to replace the Christian faith and its statements about reality, God, and the universe. Naturalism would assert that the natural phenomena of the universe are its exhaustive reality and that life has no divine, supernatural source or meaning. This created a great vacuum as we saw in the last chapter. So in the midst of the vaunted enlightenment, all types of occult spiritualism flooded in when Kant and Hegel asked the empiricists, "How do you know that you know?" Knowledge was limited to a miniscule area within "pure reason." But it would take science several centuries to realize the blow on the head that it had received then.

What had not dawned on anyone was that a giant gulf had been created between the rational objective realm of scientifically observable facts and everything invisible that has value for us (love, truth, right, wrong, good, evil, God). Man, a combination of the material and spiritual, was divided right down the middle by the Kant-Hegel system.

Kierkegaard soon came along and put on the finishing touches to the gulf to make the barrier between the physical and the spiritual totally impassable. Faith, he said, could have no relation whatsoever to the physical, the rational, the concrete. Faith was a blind leap into the unknown. As Francis Schaeffer used to suggest, this brought about modern existentialism and modern despair. A mystic, a saint, and a schizophrenic were on similar footing. Choose your "trip" and don't worry about proving it, because you can't anyway.

An Orientalist, Lucien Styrk, remarks in his anthology of Buddhistic literature, *The World of the Buddha*, that the popularity of Buddhism in the

West resulted, "not because other systems of belief have failed in their purpose but because, simply, they have been unable to coexist with those views of reality offered by science and humanistic disciplines." Man thus became the judge of reality from within outward in a Humanism that is purely man-centered. The occult is man-centered. Christianity is God-centered. Man had to assume the throne.

New gods of the West

Disposing of Christianity several hundred years ago, a number of philosophers defined what acceptable knowledge was: the "known" was observable phenomena, the method was the empirical method, and by definition it had (a priori) to shut out anything that was not in this category (These men were the British empiricists—Locke, Berkeley, and Hume—and the continental rationalists—Descartes, Leibnitz, and Spinoza. They had their differences, but it was like an in-family battle). God was thus excluded from the picture and "Science" became the new god of the West.

The Age of Reason taught that the mind of man was an all-sufficient, autonomous agent for comprehensively understanding human nature and reality. A small percentage of thinkers brought us into the Age of Reason and asserted that human intelligence could comprehend man, the world and the cosmos with adequacy.

Those who resisted this observed that the facts of life seem to tell us otherwise; the frightening brevity of life, the vastness of the world, and the limited experience of man, given his small allotment of time and space, should tell us that man is going beyond himself in so ambitious a project as to try to logically disassemble, and account for, the cosmos. The task requires an overview that is more than humanly derived. If there is a purpose behind the universe, it is too vast for us to discover or conceive; it seems like an ant trying to comprehend a Mahler symphony. The only alternative in so staggering a project is for a mind greater than the cosmos to reveal its true purpose to us; an intelligence any less in magnitude is not equipped to give us an ultimate answer.

But in the Age of Reason the transcendental supernatural basis for existence was finally thrown out. If man could not have access to God by his reason or physical experience, then God was at root defined as unknowable, if not nonexistent.

To prove that God was a myth, the irreverent Voltaire proudly averred, "if God did not exist, it would be necessary to invent him." All things knowable, the Age of Reason insisted, had to begin with man and his mind and experience. Any fact that could not meet this standard was tossed out as superstition. Science asserted "whatever my net does not catch is not fish." Yet what about those things too large and too small to fit net of science?

This anti-Christian bias of science became the dominant mode for understanding reality in the West. Its assumptions went unquestioned, even straying into religious circles (fueling the theology of doubt and skepticism that started with German "higher criticism" in the late 1800s and whose latest configuration is the Jesus Seminar).

But wait—what was science doing suddenly straying into theology? By accurate definition, any concern with the invisible-religion, ethical values, metaphysics—is not within the province of science, whose business extends no further than the observation and collation of data. Science had entered the temple

Speculations and statements about ultimate reality and meanings behind the universe are not proper to science, because science studies observable and repeatable phenomena piecemeal and from the outside. That study cannot discover the power and purpose behind reality. As C.S. Lewis remarked in *Mere Christianity*, "if there was a controlling power outside the universe, it would not show itself to us as one of the facts inside the universe—no more than the architect of a house could actually be a wall or staircase or fireplace in that house."[1]

All the same, the language of science became synonymous with the language of truth. The result is that the description of anything in scientific jargon (with apparent scientific detachment) creates an overwhelming impression of authority and authenticity. A case in point, as was mentioned earlier, is the format in which Moody presents his "data." Science is speaking here in the province of religion, and his scientific language consoles us with a religious belief in life after death (with none of the unpleasantness or demands of a biblical God, before whom men are morally accountable). People are grabbing onto it like a life raft in a pitching storm, because the other alternative that they have been faced with so long is the despair of rationalism with its universe of blind chance.

Science was transformed from a method to a faith. It went from a simple method of observation to an entire perspective about reality, which in itself was taken on faith (this is called "scientism"). At a sweep, man's most meaningful perception of himself as a mind, body, and soul created with purpose by an infinite God was denied and brushed aside.

As the Age of Reason made pronouncements about the validity of various approaches to knowledge, the arena of philosophic inquiry shrank radically from ontology, the study of the nature of being and reality, to epistemology, the theory of knowledge. The concern of thinkers shifted from the study of God and God's universe to the study of the human mind and its limitations.

Kant asked, "What can the mind know, how does it know, and how does it know that it knows?" The modern thinkers have continued to ask this same question since the time of Kant. Man as opposed to God was further advanced as the central and definitive fact in the universe. Man could touch and feel himself, and that was all that was needed to prove to most men that they existed.

Cambridge University whose legacy included some of the greatest men of the Reformation—Latimer, Tyndale, Ridley, Wilberforce, Cromwell, John Harvard—by the early 1900s had a group of intellectuals—Bertrand Russell, Alfred North Whitehead, and AJ Ayer (and in a different way Ludwig Wittgenstein)—as intent on fully unseating God as the former group sought to glorify Him. These *Logical Positivists*—philosophers of epistemology, philology, and mathematics—gloried in their own brilliance, cutting glamorous paths among the avant garde and cultural elite as the new *cause d'celebre*, radically chic and full of themselves.

Bertrand Russell, leader of the Logical Positivists at Trinity College, not only wrote the heralded *Principia Mathematica* but then wrote, *Why I am not a Christian*, shaking the faith of a great many of his generation by showing that intellectuals saw through the myth of God, a myth sought by lesser plebeian minds who are just too weak to face life without a prop. But illumined minds could take it all in and didn't need any props. Academics, like lemmings, followed suit, creating a vast wave that washed across academia well into the mid 20th century.

Intellectual-wanna-bes of that generation soon emulated the new fashion of liberated skepticism expected of true intellectuals, glorying in the accolades and the sensual rewards of not having to deal with the concept of sin. It was surely a renaissance for the human ego, some egos above others. Nothing stood in the way of their own autonomous self-expression, these secular and humanist oracles of new truth.

Bertrand Russell

By declaring God dead, man was also murdering himself and his own significance. Jean Paul Sartre was now free to declare that "man is a meaningless passion." Without God, in whose image man was made, man became no more than a fact among facts, an animal among animals, and had no more significant than a fragment of quartz or an amoeba. The public had been robbed but didn't know it.

As a result of the loss of God-guaranteed identity, man became dead matter without a soul which could be molded like putty into any shape desired by a ruling elite.

This is precisely the terrible vision that George Orwell depicted in his novel *1984* writte*n* in the forties—the totalitarianism of man taking on the responsibility of playing God and creating a nightmare in the process. History repeatedly shows that man makes a cruel and insane god; every Caesar and every dictator proves this point.

So Great a Loss

What then was the Christian view of reality that the rationalists threw out?

Man at that time knew himself as a fallen creature within a fallen universe, and both were utterly dependent upon the grace of God for stability, continuity, and comprehensibility. All of man's experience in this life was intelligible through faith in God's self-revelation in history. Life and death, good and evil, and suffering and grief were not lost in the dark, impenetrable mystery of chance and blind evolution. They were comprehended through the laws of God—such as cause and effect—as well as the sovereign purpose of God in His Creation.

In the biblical universe, certain things were given philosophically: through God's revelation we know that we live in a world of his creation which is rational and purposive. Though we do not possess the minds to comprehend it fully, we know that our minds are suited to understanding the universe in limited ways. We know that the material universe is objective and real, that time and space and causality are not illusions but part of the actual form and structure of this universe. We know that we are each known and loved individually by God and that our personalities are real and significant.

We also realize that we are morally accountable before this God and that our life actions are not random and meaningless, but significant enough to receive judgment. We are culpable for our acts—we are not just victims of an endless chain—because we were given the gift of choice, of wills that determine and act. We also have an incredible source of hope coming from the restoration of our relationship with this God. Being made in the image of this God, we also have a spiritual aspect to our nature—we have/are embodied souls. And that means our bodies are not all of who we are. Nor is love an accident. Nor is truth. It is a coherent and purposive cosmos where beauty and meaning can exist—so can evil.

It is now understandable, therefore, that when the Age of Reason uprooted this foundation, a crisis ensued. The model of the universe that man had cherished for so long was no longer assured. But it would take time for the import of this to fully hit home.

All people wish to feel that life is something more than brute chance, and death more than total annihilation. And that is exactly what they were left with when God was removed.

In a sense, the Age of Reason was "the great revolt." When a ship full of ignorant and rebellious slaves mutiny in mid sea and kill the captain and his officers, they may be able to operate the ship for a stretch. But if they are unable to read the charts and steer the ship, their successful rebellion becomes their own defeat, for eventually they will be lost, wrecked, and marooned.

Was this what happened to rationalism with its heady ambitions? Did it give us its promised utopia? The promise is still there, looming in the air like a super mart special. Science still says, "Just wait, the answer is just around the corner," but its voice is quickly losing the authority it once had.

Perhaps the problem is most clearly summed up by that brilliant journalist, the former editor of *Punch*, Malcolm Muggeridge who indeed had been at Selwyn College Cambridge when Bertrand Russell was in his prime. Muggeridge, for a time, believed the Humanist myth then recanted:

> It is difficult to resist the conclusion that there is a death wish at work at the heart of our civilization whereby our banks promote the inflation which will ruin them, our educationalists seem to create the moral and intellectual chaos which will nullify their professional purposes, our physicians invent new and more terrible diseases to replace those they have abolished, our moralists cut away the roots of all morality and our theologians dismantle the structure of belief they exist to expound and promote.[2]

Tal Brooke & Malcolm Muggeridge

After years of scathing cynicism, Muggeridge, the one-time Fabian Socialist stalwart of the Left who had glorified Bolshevism as a journalist from Moscow in the 1930s, became a Christian. He says his conversion was not at all an escape; but a most sane and rational conclusion, and it changed him from the inside out. He had learned that the liberal utopian dream had been a lie. In the final years of his life he and I became friends (he discovered a copy of ***Avatar of Night*** in Calcutta and had some very good things to say about it).

Escaping the Vacuum

There is not a scientist alive who can look out to the distant galaxies and quasars, which are millions of light years away, and then look at the teeming microbes beneath his feet and explain how they got there. The scientists do not know; they are still theorizing. Their best attempt so far at an explanation is that it is all somehow a kind of an accident, which is a paltry response to an immense question.

All that the philosophy of science has done is left us with a head full of questions and a spiritual identity crisis in our souls. How could the scientistic philosophy fully satisfy our needs if there is a whole spiritual side to our nature? It does not matter whether science recognizes this or not; it is there. Yet through the lens of science we have played a charade, pretending to be what we are not; like the proverbial mental patient, we can freeze in the garden and pretend to be corn stalks, but after enough rain and cold, and after we have missed a few meals, we will soon become fidgety and even more clearly betray our real nature. We are not corn stalks any more than we are just chemicals woven into vast DNA strands. So we fight the vacuum left by science because it goes against our nature. The problem is that once we have been persuaded (or seduced) into abandoning reason—one of the factors that makes us in the image of God—we enter the same dangerous terrain once held by Babylon that God warned against.

The concrete result is the Postmodern physicist who "throws the I Ching," the occult Chinese book of fortune, and the pragmatist who is willing to be guided by the invisible channeled revelation of some spirit guide, as evidenced by Kubler-Ross and Salem.

The West has thus regressed to the forbidden land of occultic practices which rationalism sought to abolish. Man, again asserting himself as more than a bag of chemicals or a piece of merchandise, is finding meaning again, but it is through the gnosticism of the ancient world—and this may be an even stronger delusion than Rationalism.

If there is some kind of cosmic malignant intelligence, as the Bible states, then the magic trick took place when modern man leaped from the checkmated position of Rationalist despair to the extra rational free fall of blind faith. Without any spiritual guidelines, man is now truly vulnerable in a wholly new way. He has returned to a primitive inner-directed religious subjectivism—from spiritualism, to pantheism, and even devil worship. Truly, this equation begins to look more and more like some diabolical tour de force.

The only final alternative left in our wide search is the transcendent, personal God of the universe, who ordained all order and at times intervened in history to provide us with knowledge and revelation, which we in our own efforts could never uncover. This is the ultimate Author of the Bible and the sovereign Creator.

14

The Eternal Word

The grass withers,
the flower fades;
but the word of our God
shall stand for ever (Isaiah. 40:8).

Above such questions as—Did Christ live? Are there miracles? and, Has the Bible prophesied the future again and again from one age to another? The basic question is: Apart from the lineage of prophets and scribes who did the actual speaking and recording, "Is God the ultimate author of the Bible and is it a reliable communication from Him?"

It certainly refers to itself as the unique Word of God, unlike any other book in existence. It is also a miracle, for the history of this supernatural book pales any drama in history. Indeed, the Bible stands at the apex of history, different in *kind* from all other books ever written (with enough amazing facts about it to fill a *Guiness Book of World Records)*. Yet few have bothered to do more than flip through it in a whole lifetime. Yet they invoke the standard array of pat answers when questioned about it. Public ignorance is staggering.

Perhaps we should ponder why and how such a revelation should be given to the human race in the first place.

It certainly makes sense that if there really is a God who created the universe, then it is within His power to actually enter history and reveal Himself. And he would certainly have a reason to reveal himself if his creation had a purpose that required his explaining—especially if his creation, man, couldn't figure it out on his own.

If man had a special purpose, then God would be negligent if man were left alone to grope in the dark and puzzle things out for himself, especially if it were beyond man's capacities to arrive at ultimate solutions.

From our human perspective, we could say that the complex creation around us plus our abilities seem to testify to the fact that we have significance. We are more than just a bag of chemicals. Rather, if our intelligence, will, and emotions are more than haphazard results of creation, then they really do have a purpose. Through all of our faculties, we can receive and understand communications about the meaning and purpose of the whys and wherefores of existence itself. God could and would reach from the infinite down to the finite, cross the gulf that we could never cross, and directly intervene in our world.

This is exactly what the Bible claims has happened. God intervened in history, and the Bible is the record of that intervention. Man did not just perform some religious rite and summon so great a One as God into speaking. Rather, God himself purposed his communications in his own way and on his own terms, which has always been a problem to many.

God chose special individuals of incredible purity and integrity through whom He would give his Word. His prophets were utterly different from the mediums and psychics of Babylon and the East, both in simple, humble, human character, and in morals. Rather than receiving subjective inner experiences, his prophets had the inner quickening of the fire of the Holy Spirit; they were enlivened with active and not passive

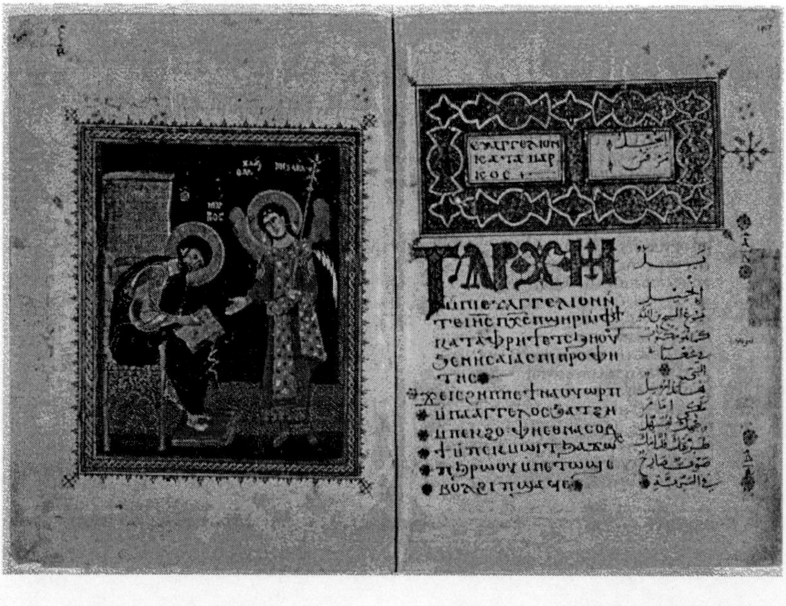

minds. They felt the awesome power of their living God, and they were 100 percent accurate in what they said and predicted, with miracles occurring time and time again to support their words. Above all, they testified that their revelations were from a transcendent, holy God, before whom all they could do was to fall upon their faces. They never even hinted at a divine-within experience or a higher-self experience.

Human Limitations & the need for Revelation

Why the need for revelation? Again, because even if man had a billion years of uninterrupted laboratory investigation, and had broken down all the material and mechanical facts behind the physical universe, he would still be ignorant of the much higher qualities of spiritual reality.

He could not squeeze good and evil out of a frozen charge of energy. Man would be approaching the whole problem in an upside-down fashion. Not that there is not a clear continuum tying the physical to the spiritual, but simply, from man's point of view, he lacks the resources to tie them together (as we have seen from the Rationalists, then Kant, and Kierkegaard).

Something lesser cannot transcend itself to understand the greater. An idiot will never understand Stephen Hawking's theories of the event horizon of black holes or James Joyce's ***Ulysses*** (which are above normal intelligence levels to say the least). And on a more accurate level of analogy, an ant on some table top will not be able to understand Beethoven's 5th Symphony because we have an infinite ontological gulf here. **And certainly man's billion-year-old laboratory would never go beyond the universe to peer into the character of an infinite God.** We must understand this in order to comprehend the need for revelation.

We have established the human need for God's revelation. Having seen that need, let us briefly examine the substance of the revelation, the record, and its format. F.F. Bruce, a foremost Bible scholar, defines the range of the Bible:

> The Bible, at first sight, appears to be a collection of literature—mainly Jewish. If we enquire into the circumstances under which the various Biblical documents were written, we find that they were written at intervals over a space of nearly 1400 years. The writers wrote in various lands, from Italy in the west of Mesopotamia and possibly Persia in the east. The writers themselves were a heterogeneous number of

> people, not only separated from each other by hundreds of years and hundreds of miles, but belonging to the most diverse walks of life. In their ranks we have kings, herdsmen, soldiers, legislators, fishermen, statesmen, courtiers, priests and prophets, a tentmaking Rabbi and a Gentile physician, not to speak of others of whom we know nothing apart from the writings they have left us. The writings themselves belong to a great variety of literary types. They include history, law (civil, criminal, ethical, ritual, sanitary), religious poetry, didactic treatises, lyric poetry, parable and allegory, biography, personal correspondence, personal memoirs and diaries, in addition to the distinctively Biblical types of prophecy and apocalyptic.
>
> For all that, the Bible is not simply an anthology; there is a unity which binds the whole together. An anthology is compiled by an anthologist, but no anthologist compiled the Bible.[1]

What stands out in all that testifies against merely human authorship is the profound unity of thought in the Bible. Josh McDowell, after citing the above passage in his own book, recounts:

> A representative of the Great Books of The Western World came to my house recruiting salesmen for their series. He spread out the chart of the Great Books of The Western World series. He spent five minutes talking to us about . . . the series and we spent an hour and a half talking to him about the Greatest Book.
>
> I challenged him to take just 10 of the authors, all from one walk of life, one generation, one place, one time, one mood, one continent, one language, and just one controversial subject (the Bible speaks on hundreds with harmony and agreement). Then I asked him: "Would they (the authors) agree?" He paused and then replied, "No!" "What would you have?" I retorted. Immediately he said, "A conglomeration." Two days later he committed his life to Christ {the theme of the Bible).[2]

The format alone of the Bible displays incredible unity. The Bible speaks single-mindedly from scores of people, recording historical events as it teaches, which shows that it was tangibly given across time. Is this important? Yes, the Bible's regard for tangible history is an important philosophical comment on the nature of reality. As opposed to the Hindu teaching of maya, which says *everything* is an illusion, God proclaims his creation to be fully real. And there is more.

Historical and Archeological Evidence

History offers evidence of real events, which a reasonable individual would require in making a decision of faith; this is not a blind leap. Our minds require some kind of tangible knowledge that biblical events actually occurred. Can we ascertain this?

Consider that in America today we all stand upon a foundation of prior events in history—civilizations have come and gone; wars, eras, fashions, inventions, and great men have preceded us, all of them directly affecting where we are right now. We know that America had a Civil War, for we have all kinds of written records about it, from the memoirs of soldiers and their families to government documents and records in the archives. Also, Civil War ruins, monuments, relics, coins, guns, cannons, maps, and such evidence as the names of streets testify that the war really occurred. That war had an effect on where America is today, and other events that were as real as the Civil War just as tangibly brought about the war and the events that happened prior to it. Those earlier events, such as the American Revolution and the voyage of Columbus, left their marks upon us as well. America did not just spring out of nowhere; it emerged from an historical progression of events, and there is plenty of evidence today that they took place. The same historical argument holds true for Christ's appearance.

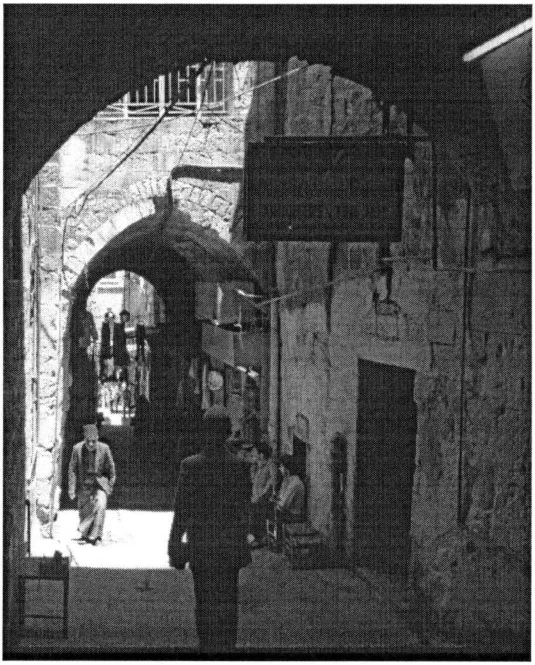

Too much evidence of the Christ event exists historically, geographically, and archaeologically to deny it. To deny the evidence would be to deny all of ancient history, including the Roman Empire. In Israel today there are

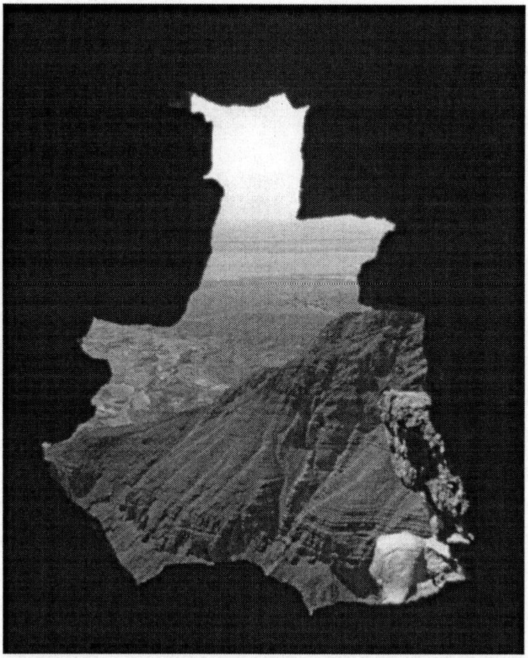

endless documents, Dead Sea Scrolls, Jewish records, ruins, coins, and other numerous items.

Historians alive in the time of Christ supply accounts of Him and his followers. Roman historian Tacitus [born A.D. 53) says that Nero blamed the burning of Rome on the Christians, and that it was Pontius Pilate who put Christ to death; Flavius Josephus, a Jewish historian, mentions numerous miracles of Christ in his famous *Antiquities* (xviii. 33), written early in the second century; and Thallus, another Roman historian, blamed the universally accepted darkening of the sky at Christ's crucifixion on "an eclipse."

Sir William A. Ramsay, the famous archaeologist, referred to the Book of Acts as "an authority for the topography, antiquities, and society of Asia Minor." But the greatest historical sources of the life and times of Christ are detailed in the New Testament.

However, most people dismiss the New Testament records as biased and therefore invalid. But this argument of "bias" is an argument that historiography will not tolerate.

The Rules of Evidence

An eyewitness account is an eyewitness account; the legal profession stands on this. Because the New Testament is a primary eyewitness document, judicial evidence can be brought to bear on it in legal inquiry.

A number of the most brilliant legal minds have sought to use judicial evidence to depose once and for all the New Testament record, especially the resurrection account. One of these men, Simon Greenleaf, was the famous Royall professor of law at the Harvard Law School and succeeded Justice Story as the Dane professor of law. Greenleaf's outstanding contribution to the field of law was a work entitled *A Treatise on the Law of Evidence*, which H. Knott, a legal authority, says "is still considered the single greatest authority on evidence in the entire literature of legal procedure."

Greenleaf's conclusion after submitting the New Testament accounts to the most rigorous juridical analysis was that the Gospels had an impenetrable defense that would hold up in any court of law. Greenleaf became a believer. His extensive inquiry is entitled *An Examination of the Testimony of the Four Evangelists by the Rules of Evidence Administered in the Courts of justice.*[3]

By legal procedure, the New Testament is indisputable. But one might still ask, "Yes, but how are we sure that these biblical documents have not been tampered with over the ages? How do they compare to the originals?"

First, the time gap between the writing of the Gospels and the ascent of Christ was no more than the gap separating us from the era of the 60's. So the Gospels were completely contemporary, just as today scores of eyewitnesses are living who saw the 60s, and numerous highly detailed accounts have been written about this wild decade, including rock music and a host of other stuff. I certainly remember the era, for I too lived through it! To me it all feels like only yesterday.

In his own day, Peter the apostle said, "For we did not follow cleverly devised tales when we made known to you the power and coming of our Lord Jesus Christ, but we were eyewitnesses of His majesty" (2 Pet. 1:16, NASB).

When Peter wrote his accounts, scores of eyewitnesses were alive who could have challenged historical falsehoods and said, "Everybody knows that the Sanhedrin discounted Christ's resurrection. Why, they paraded the corpse through the streets of Jerusalem." But people in the apostle's day could not say this. If the resurrection had been disproven by the authorities of the day, certainly Peter's preaching in Jerusalem itself, only months after the crucifixion, would not have resulted in the conversion of over two thousand in a single afternoon. The common people knew that something incredible was happening. Contradictory evidence would have stopped Christianity and the New Testament documents right then and there.

The Book of Acts cites that at one point five hundred people saw the

resurrected Christ in full view.

J. N.D. Anderson, a professor of law, says,

> Think of the number of witnesses, over 500. Think of the character of the witnesses, men and women who gave the world the highest ethical teaching it has ever known, and who even on the testimony of enemies lived it out in their lives. Think of the psychological absurdity of picturing a little band of defeated cowards cowering in an upper room one day and a few days later transformed into a company that no persecution could silence—and then attempting to attribute this dramatic change to nothing more convincing than a miserable fabrication they were trying to foist upon the world. That simply would not make sense."[4]

There is another thing to consider. No one will proceed with a willful deception when it involves his life. Hosts of the early Christians were painfully put to death, martyred. This makes it clearer why the contemporaries of the New Testament writers did not refute their writings, and how these eyewitness accounts could be written in their day and stand. But we are still left with the question asked earlier: How do today's New Testament records match the original ones?

The Ancient Writs Compared

A.T. Robertson, a manuscript authority, says, "There are some 8,000 manuscripts of the Latin Vulgate and at least 1,000 for the other early versions. Add over 4,000 Greek manuscripts and we have 13,000 manuscript copies of portions of the New Testament. Besides all of this, much of the New Testament Can be reproduced from the quotations of the early Christian writers."[5]

Comparing today's best translations with the most ancient records, we find no essential differences. Sir Frederick G. Kenyon, another manuscript authority, states, "The interval then between the dates of the original composition and the earliest extant evidence becomes so small as to be in fact negligible, and the last foundation of any doubt that the scriptures have come down to us substantially as they were written has now been removed. Both the authenticity and the general integrity of the books of the New Testament may be regarded as finally established."[6]

Various copies from over the past seventeen hundred years have had no essential differences. Indeed, the remarkable preservation of the New Testament seems to be exactly as Christ himself predicted, "Heaven and earth will pass away, but My words will not pass away" (Luke 21:33,

NASB). Yet should this surprise us when we consider that if God can hold the galaxies in their courses, He can surely preserve his revelation. The Word of God has remained miraculously intact over the ages; and when one considers some of the attempts throughout history to blot it out, the entire picture becomes even more incredible.

So far we have seen the Bible's incredible range, that it speaks with a single mind, that history and archaeology support it, that its internal evidence would stand in any court of law, and that the manuscripts have been preserved with incredible accuracy.

Now we must consider another aspect of the Bible, which points even more obviously to its unique distinction of being a miraculous book: prophecy. In hundreds of places, the Bible has foretold events with absolute accuracy, often centuries before they occurred. No other book in the world can claim this. The advent of Christ was prophesied in the Old Testament hundreds of years before his birth. Predictive prophecy further says that a supreme, all-knowing intelligence is behind the Bible.

The most incredible prophecies concern the very cornerstone of the Bible, Jesus Christ. Written in great detail centuries before his birth, they state where and when he would be born; of what lineage; and his purpose, mission, death, and ascent. The staggering fact is that 332 specific Old Testament prophecies are about Christ.

Equally incredible is what this means if one considers the exact fulfillment of these prophecies in terms of the science of mathematical probability; they constitute an impossibility if left to blind chance, and a divine miracle if fulfilled, as they have been.

Mathematician Peter Stoner reports that the chance of just 48 of the Old Testament prophecies coming true by accident is 1 in 10^{157}', a number so vast that it is greater than the number of estimated atoms in the entire universe. This constitutes a miracle. The common rebuttal, however, is: But how do we know that these prophecies were not written after Christ, and after the fact? The answer is: because the Jews and their Bible-based civilization existed for centuries before Christ. Their entire life structure and orientation were based on the Old Testament laws and prophecies, from the writings of Moses, the psalms of David, and the proverbs of Solomon, to the prophecies of Isaiah and Ezekiel.

How do we know that the Old Testament prophecies preceded Christ? Here is absolute proof: "The Septuagint, the Greek translation of the Hebrew scripture, was completed in the reign of Ptolemy Philadelphus

The Isaiah Scroll in Jerusalem

(285-246 B.C.). It is rather obvious that if you have a Greek translation in 250 B.C., then you had to have the Hebrew text from which it was written in 250 B.C. This will suffice to indicate that there was at least a 250-year gap between the prophecies being written down and their fulfillment in the Person of Christ."[7]

What about the corruption of the Old Testament text? Consider this: If a Hebrew scribe in the ancient world miss copied even a single letter on a given day, he would bum that particular parchment, leave the school, bathe in a river, and pray the remainder of the day. Everything he wrote was read and reread for errors by rabbis and over viewers.

When the Dead Sea Scrolls were discovered, they were found to be almost two thousand years old. Obviously they had remained untouched. Previously, the oldest manuscript of Isaiah, known as the Masoretic text, dated back to A.D. 916. The Dead Sea Scrolls are a thousand years older, and the Masoretic text had a thousand extra years of transcription beyond the Dead Sea Scrolls. When the two texts were compared, they were essentially identical. Geisler and Nix state in their general introduction to the Bible that between the two Isaiah scrolls, "'in one chapter of 166 words, there is only one word (three letters) in question after a thousand years of transmission—and this word does not significantly change the meaning of the passage."[8] The Old Testament, like the New Testament, has been transmitted essentially without error over the ages.

To get to the heart of the matter, when you see the immense effort put into a book like the Bible, you can conclude that at the very least it is trying to make a point, and that not to consider its communications would be genuine foolishness.

Revealed sufficiently in the Bible's revelations are the character of God, the scheme of creation and ultimate reality, absolute spiritual values, and the coming history of the ages as it is progressively unfolds. As mentioned earlier, at its cornerstone—where all prophecy points—is the advent of Christ, the expression of the written eternal Word as the living Word, the ultimate intervention of God in history. He is the messianic concept of "Emmanuel" or "God with us." As the God-man, Christ is God's final revelation of his own essential nature, a fact large enough for anyone to comprehend. This fact of Christ's deity became the stumbling block of the world, yet Christ is the ultimate bridge between man and the eternal God. No other route, no other alternative, will be given. The great mystery lies in the ransom sacrifice, the final release for many. The crucifixion is the ultimate release from the power of death.

A Mystery Revealed

In every gospel, in chapter after chapter, Christ is found claiming incredible things for himself, unlike anyone who has ever existed. Christ claimed the power to forgive sins, He controlled the forces of nature, He claimed authority over venerable tradition, and He boldly predicted his own death, resurrection and return to judge the world. Eventually the authorities had enough of it and put Him to death for blasphemy. Jesus was not unwilling to die, for He saw death as part of His redeeming mission, but He reiterated time and again that death would not hold Him, and that His resurrection would decisively prove His claims.

The one nation that would not take a man's claim to deity lightly was ancient Israel, which feared and venerated the names of their God (Jehovah, Elohim, etc.). If a man were to try to set himself up and pretend the role, Israel was not the place to do it; Greece, Rome, Egypt, or Persia, perhaps, but not Israel. As He led an utterly sober and blameless life, Christ would describe himself in the identical Old Testament language used for God alone: "Before Abraham was, I am" (John 8:58); "He who has seen Me has seen the Father" (John 14:9, NASB); and, like God, He was referred to as the Creator (John 1:3), the Savior, the Judge, the Light of the world, the Glory of God, the Redeemer, the Forgiver of sins, and the Alpha and Omega. All of these are attributed to God in the Old Testament. The Jews knew that only One was deserving of worship, God. And Christ received worship from a leper, from the apostle Thomas, and others. The Epistle to the Hebrews says that even the very angels adored and worshiped Christ (Heb. 1:6), an honor that was out of the question for a mere mortal, a mere created being. When Stephen the martyr was stoned to death, he looked up and prayed to Christ to receive his spirit (Acts 7:59).

It seems evident at this point that Christ's claim to deity was very real, and the implications of what this means have never been put better than in the words of C.S. Lewis:

> I am trying here to prevent anyone saying the really foolish thing that people often say about Him: 'I'm ready to accept Jesus as a great moral teacher, but I don't accept His claim to be God.' That is the one thing we must not say. A man who was merely a man and said the sort of things Jesus said would not be a great moral teacher. He would either be a lunatic—on a level with the man who says he is a poached egg—or else he would be the Devil of Hell. You must make your choice. Either this man was, and is, the Son of God: or else a madman or something worse."[10]

Now it is time to finally find out what Christ and Scripture tell us about death: what it really is, when it started, what transpires after physical death, what the Bible says about escape from the final clutches of death, and the hope that God has made available to fallen man.

15

The Eternal Day

C.S. Lewis, a gifted scholar, professor at Oxford and Cambridge, and man of letters, who once described himself, converted while in his forties, as "the most reluctant and dejected convert in all of England," said something once that pierced my heart. Having just returned from India, I was in London reading a talk entitled "The Weight of Glory," given by Lewis at Oxford's Magdalene college chapel. The words, I would learn, were not the wild, unbridled theologizings of an overdeveloped literary imagination trying to compensate for a meager exposure to biblical knowledge; rather, they were based on a profound and systematic awareness of the permutations of Scripture. Lewis's literary genius propelled these truths with a vividness lacking in many theologians.

> It is a serious thing to live in a society of possible gods and goddesses, to remember that the dullest and most uninteresting person you can talk to may one day be a creature which, if you saw it now, you would be strongly tempted to worship, or else a horror and a corruption such as you now meet, if at all, only in a nightmare. All day long we are, in some degree, helping each other to one or other of these destinations . . . . There are no ordinary people. You have never talked to a mere mortal.
>
> Nations, cultures, arts, civilizations these are mortal, and their life is to ours as the life of a gnat. But it is immortals whom we joke with, work with, marry, snub, and exploit—immortal horrors or everlasting splendors. [1]

If I had left Hyde Park and walked to the borough of London known as Westminster, I would have seen etched on an old wall that great confession of faith drawn up four hundred years before Lewis by that assembly of Christians who carefully proof texted, with a jealous reverence, their confession of faith, the Westminster Confession.

The Westminster Assembly had such a high regard for Scripture that they dared not stray even a jot or a tittle from the clear declarations of biblical revelation. They would add or subtract nothing from Scripture's declaration, for they knew that by doing so they would jeopardize their very souls for eternity (see Rev. 22:19). They dared not handle "the word of God deceitfully" (2 Cor. 4:2).

The Reality of Death

Had I read what they had written, I would have found "The Eternal Day," in chapter 32 of the confession, where men become "immortal horrors or everlasting splendors." The following excerpt from the great confession pieces together the key biblical verses on what happens when we die.

> The bodies of men, after death, return to dust, and see corruption: (Gen. 3:19; Acts 13:36) but their souls, which neither die nor sleep, having an immortal substance, immediately return to God who gave them: (Luke 23:43; Eccles. 12:7) the souls of the righteous, being then made perfect in holiness, are received in the highest heavens, where they behold the face of God, in light and glory, waiting for the full redemption of their bodies. (Heb. 12:23; Ii Cot. 5:1, 6, 8; Phil. 1:23; Acts 3:21; Eph. 4:10; Rom. 8:23). And the souls of the wicked are cast into hell; where they remain in torments and utter darkness, reserved to the judgment of the great day. (Luke 16:23, 24; Acts 1:25; Jude 6, 7; I Pet. 3:19). Beside these two places, for souls separated from the bodies, the Scripture acknowledgeth none.
>
> At the last day, such as are found alive shall not die, but be changed: (I The s s. 4:17; I Cor. 15:51,52) and all the dead shall be raised up, with the selfsame bodies, and none other (although with different qualities), which shall be united again to their souls forever (John 5:25-29; Acts 24:15; Job 19:26, 27; Dan. 12:2; I Cor. 15:42-44).
>
> The bodies of the unjust shall, by the power of Christ, be raised to dishonor; the bodies of the just, by His Spirit, unto honor; and be made conformable to His own glorious body. (Acts 24:15; John 5:25-29; I Cor. 15:43; Phil. 3:21).[2]

This banner of the great Reformation, which characterized the era of Calvin, Luther, Whitefield, and a host of great men, is a most careful distilling of the foundations of the Christian faith. Chapter 33, the last chapter, compasses the final judgment. Like the rest of the confession, it is derived from a clear lining up of hundreds of key Scriptures, according to context, intent, and meaning. Since it pertains to all of creation, it is wise to read it:

> God hath appointed a day, wherein He will judge the world, in righteousness, by Jesus Christ (Acts 17:31), to whom all power and judgment is given of the Father. (John 5:22, 27). In which day, not only the apostate angels shall be judged (Jude 6; II Pet. 2:4), but likewise all persons that have lived upon earth shall appear before the tribunal of Christ, to give an account of their thoughts, words, and deeds; and to receive according to what they have done in the body, whether good or evil (II Cor. 5:10; Eccles. 12:14; Rom. 14:10, 12; Matt. 12:36, 37).
>
> The end of God's appointing this day is for the manifestation of the glory of His mercy, in the eternal salvation of the elect; and of His justice, in the damnation of the reprobate, who are wicked and disobedient. For then shall the righteous go into everlasting life, and receive the fullness of joy and refreshing, which shall come from the presence of the Lord: but the wicked, who know not God, and obey not the gospel of Jesus Christ, shall be cast into eternal torments, and be punished with everlasting destruction from the presence of the Lord, and from the glory of His power (Matt. 25:31-46; Rom. 2:5,6; Rom. 9:22, 23; Matt. 25:21; Acts 3:19; II Thess. 1:7-10; Mark 9:48)?

These "hard truths" are so weighty that as a rule people cover their ears in protest to escape its impact. It is the one fact of Scripture that people detest the most and try to forget as quickly as possible. Yet no evangelist is honest if he wishes to push people gently into the Kingdom of heaven with tinsel and trinkets while ignoring or being ashamed of the eternal day. It is there, and none can ignore it, for it will come as surely as the rising sun. The tendency to banish it by warping it into a stereotype and then utterly despising it is common. I did that most of my life. Yet often I got the most unsettled feeling when the remnants of my conscience, which I had all but subdued, would occasionally rise up to protest. Meanwhile, my mind raced to find viable alternatives, saying, " I thought I had disposed of you once and for all; yet you come back to haunt me like a ghost."

The ultimate solution is not the Zen Koan, the primal scream, the up-front commune style, the transactional group's total encounter, or the transcendent samadhi; it is to look directly at the bare facts of God. It is the ultimate epistemological problem. I spent a painful childhood observing sophisticates of the adult world sidestep this problem with some of the most complex diversions, stratagems, and psychological games. What the human mind can devise to escape this reality is almost awesome. Because this, far above the ego death of the East, requires a true change of oneself and true humility, it is known as "conversion." Few are willing to give up their own private claims on their lives, and they will not admit the tenacity with which they are holding on to what they want their lives to be.

Aldous Huxley once exemplified this impenitence by saying that he never really had an intellectual problem with Christianity; he had a moral one, for he did not deny the facts or the inevitable sense they made. He was offended by how the morality curtailed his freedoms. Likewise, there may be a thousand synods whose aim it is to change the simple truth and evolve some new insight; there may be a new papal bull or some inner echelon which claims special revelation. But the fact remains, "The word of our God endures forever" (Isa. 40:8, TEV). The pages of Scripture are open, plain for all to see. If we look at all of the major confessions regarding the eternal day, they fully agree. Why? It is like a logical syllogism. God has made sure the propositions of Scripture can hold only one true configuration, whether analyzed prayerfully or run through a computer. The eternal day always emerges.

The only way to knock the configuration out of shape is to symbolize everything, as Paul Tillich and Rudolf Bultmann have, or to say that the biblical source is invalid and therefore open to private editorializing, at which point one takes a few select bits of Scripture willy-nilly to prove anything he wants. With a black enough editorial pencil, one can syncretize Christianity with anything.

Yet the mind uses other tricks to obscure the truth; the caricature is the most popular. (like Moody mockingly reminding us of angels and harps?) For example, someone says to himself, God truly did a wonderful thing by creating a cosmos of so many parsecs of intergalactic space, with distant quasars and infinite stars. When I picture the final judgment, my imagery constantly encompasses something like the local high school auditorium, with someone like the principal sitting center stage under a bare light bulb, beneath mold-covered curtains, while looking out at a most unimpressive assortment of people. Perhaps on the sidelines are a few kids made up as angels, with (you guessed it) harps, sequins, gossamer robes, and metallic bronze face cream.

We think of the cosmos, and our minds leap out forever; we think of the eternal day, and we picture it as occurring at the local civic center. Since the vision is not feasible, we reject the whole concept as primitive. We have just dealt deceitfully with the Word of God.

Such stereotypes have so deeply invaded our minds that to see beyond them requires true Christian enlightenment. For one thing, it means discarding a host of sixteenth-century paintings which we mentally overlay on Scripture. But in the process we must not deny the report of Scripture and gnosticize it into a higher mystical message. Paul anticipated this problem in his battle against the Gnostics. The apostle was most literal:

> But if there is no resurrection of the dead, then Christ has not been raised; if Christ has not been raised, then our preaching is in vain and your faith is in vain. We are even found to be misrepresenting God, because we testified of God that he raised Christ, whom he did not raise if it is true that the dead are not raised. For if the dead are not raised, your faith is futile and you are still in your sins. Then those also who have fallen asleep in Christ have perished. If for this life only we have hoped in Christ, we are of all men most to be pitied (1 Cor. 15:13-19, RSV).

Paul was not dealing with Vedanta's impersonal Godhead, Brahman, or hazy balls of light or disembodied beings of light. He was talking about the resurrected Christ, to whom Thomas physically touched then cried out, "My Lord and my God" (John 20:28). If Christ were a ball of light, that is how he would have appeared to his waiting disciples and to the crowd of five hundred. We must realize that there is something of far greater immensity than balls of light in the plan of God's new heaven. We have to compass the fact of "glorified bodies" in a context far more splendid than we have ever experienced here on earth. The problem does not lie in the revelation of God, but in our ability to visualize. Paul made this clear with the words, "Eye hath not seen, nor ear heard, neither have entered into the heart of man, the things which God hath prepared for them that love him" (1 Cor. 2:9).

Scripture has told us something; it is beyond us to visualize the eternal day, as beyond us as a blind man trying to picture the three primary colors and their infinite variations, not to speak of the Mogul Gardens of Kashmir. For that matter, nor can an ant comprehend Mahler's Tenth Symphony, scoping the vast range of feeling and complexity from the light violins to symphonic thunder, from pathos to adoration. Perhaps its antennae feel a thunderous rumble like that of a stampeding herd of cattle, but that is far from the sublime heart of Mahler's genius. So it is with us and eternity.

Therefore, what we have is a fundamental question regarding the nature of ultimate reality. In one scenario creation will groan and travail forever, only finding release in the realm of the spirit, with good and evil coexisting, endless Chicagos passing by, civilizations replacing civilizations, a million dictatorships coming and going, and Lake Erie being filtered and re purified endless times (if the world goes on as it is, its decay is indefinite, according to the second law of thermodynamics).

Or the One who made it must change all that exists to make it other than what it is. If we deny matter and call it evil, if we opt for the realm of the spirit as did the Gnostics whom Paul opposed, as do the spiritualists, we are proclaiming a definite view concerning material reality. "It must be transcended," we are saying.

But the Bible says no. Material creation fell at a terrible price. God made the material universe and declared it "good," but he is not finished; the drama is not over yet. He can and will change His travailing creation, as he promised, within the twinkling of an eye. "It is good," the Bible says, not the accident of a half-baked plan. True, man has mangled it, but look at the luminous green of a tropical leaf, the Alps of Austria, or the emerald shores of Malabar and tell me that the prototypes from which they come are evil, an expensive accident. Even after millennia of creation being in third gear, according to the biblical model, and even though these are shadows of the original types, they still take your breath away. Some say the Creator goofed? No, man goofed way back in history through a fatal choice.

Either creation will groan and travail forever, only finding release in the realm of the spirit, or God is deeply serious about his purpose to intervene in the created universe at the appointed time and change everything in the most radical way.

This could not be any more clear than in the famous epistle of the apostle Peter who says,

> It is not that he is dilatory about keeping his own promise as some men seem to think; the fact is that he is very patient with you. He has no wish that any man should be destroyed; he wishes that all men should find the way to repentance. Yet the day of the Lord will come as unexpectedly as a thief. In that day the heavens will vanish in a tearing blast, the very elements will disintegrate in heat and the earth and all its works will disappear (2 Pet. 3:9, 10, Phillips).

This matter of the new creation is discussed many times. The new creation follows the destruction of the old. But the question arises, Who will make it through the sieve? Will microbes, drug shooting galleries and porno parlors hustle their way through with a sheepish smile? Not likely.

The prospect of the new creation is staggering. What we have seen in only a mere glimpse of Eden will appear with manifest power, stretching across eternity, a symphony of matter and spirit unlike anything we know, in total congress with the eternal, spotless, and perfect God, through Christ, the cornerstone of the created universe.

What of tears and lamentation? No more. What of bloated bodies in the Hudson River? You've heard it—the ten-year-old girl sitting on her Beverly Hills porch watching her cat. The next minute a van pulls up and hustles her away to New York to be in a porno white-slave ring, where she is raped and then butchered (it is happening now). Later, her body is found bleached white in the docks of Hoboken. Never again. How God hates that! Do you think he is jesting when he speaks of hell?

What of the cancers, poisons, pus-spewing wounds of our race, with its secret, burning inner cankers, its God-hating blindness and cruelties, its complicated truth-denying games? Do you not know that since man's fall, God has pronounced the sentence, "The [human] heart is deceitful above all things, and desperately wicked: who can know it?" (Jer. 17:9). So you're a good guy? A deep enough scalpel will show the Dr. Jekyll and Mr. Hyde nature of the most decent citizen. Beneath the whitewashed tomb is the most grotesque distortion of perfection. Will the Mr. Hyde in you make it through the sieve? If so, why did the Messiah come into the world to go through infinite agony? That is a deep question. Have you really considered it?

A slag heap will be banished across an infinite void, and then forgotten forever by the Godhead. Though a void, it will not be an impersonal state, for it will most definitely contain personalities-those to whom God, love, truth, and goodness were a blotch across the sky. In the end, they will be given their own domain. As self-proclaimed gods of their own universe, they will reap the fruits of their own willful autonomy.' Of unending remorse and pain, for "the smoke of their torment ascendeth up for ever" (Rev. 14:11). Surely you have read of these people from Dickens to Tom Woolfe, and you've seen many of their names in the *New York Times*. They are all around you. Indeed, even now you may be in their ranks, if the Mr. Hyde nature in you has not yet been purged by the grace of God. Mr. Hydes do not pass into eternity to reign with God.

Consider the Word of God:

> Then I saw a great white throne and him who sat upon it; from his presence earth and sky fled away, and no place was found for them. And I saw the dead, great and small, standing before the throne, and books were opened. Also another book was opened, which is the book of life.

> And the dead were judged by what was written in the books, by what they had done. And the sea gave up the dead in it, Death and Hades gave up the dead in them, and all were judged by what they had done. Then Death and Hades were thrown into the lake of fire. This is the second death, the lake of fire; and if any one's name was not found written in the book of life, he was thrown into the lake of fire (Rev. 20:11-15, RSV).

Is it fair or right to minimize the dark realities of judgment and the terrible fate of those who have cut themselves off from God, especially when Jesus Christ himself talked hell in 38 different places in the Gospel of Matthew alone? I am not being your friend if I say, "Don't worry" as you are about to do the equivalent of hiring a serial killer to help around the house and baby sit, all because I don't want to spoil your mood.

Those who have judged the Bible and mythologized hell to ease their minds have done the equivalent. They are telling you a different story than the one the Bible proclaims in its serious warnings. And it is a high stakes gamble. In hundreds of places in both the Old Testament and the New Testament, God speaks of Gehenna and Sheol. These warnings are said in the tone of a concerned father who sees his small child squatting over a spiderweb, playfully fingering a black widow. The child can die in seconds and if the dad is screaming, there is import behind the emotion—it is to protect in the face of terrible danger. If you declare the biblical warnings a mere myth, you are resting your soul on your own huge intuitive proclamation.

Yet the Bible is not a flash in the pan that came and went like a thousand fads. It is not a novel twist or a new breakthrough or a new peculiarity. Like Christ, it is "the same yesterday and today and for ever" (Heb. 13:8, RSV). (Just think, the very date on your birth certificate, or on your newspaper, is based on the advent of Christ.) If it were less, it could not be absolute truth. Yet people who summarily dismiss the Bible—which has survived over 20 centuries and turned civilizations on their heads—even though they have never read it, will rest their eternal souls (and future bodies) on a "discovery" of Seth or on John Doe's "death experience." It is selective gullibility.

Think of it, someone grabs a thin, new, little book, and believes John Doe's death account above the words of the great men of God who lived across a span of many centuries, who saw world empires come and go, and whom God chose to be his mouthpieces. Those prophets and apostles often worked miracles and their moral quality of life was astounding. A modern reader will question the Bible in an instant, but he will gladly gulp down every tidbit about astral planes, beings of light and spirit guides spoken through a lisping medium who glories perversely about being in the limelight—such as showboating on *Oprah Winfrey*. Never would it occur to our lay reader that his faith rides on a far more flimsy string than is warranted, and not a single John Doe lay in a tomb for four days, as did Lazarus, in the stench of decaying flesh.

Raise a Lazarus and we have a miracle. But with John Doe the needle floated, the EEG floated, the watch ticked away from three to ten minutes, and clinicians yelled, "Dead." Old John revived and they proclaimed in all their wisdom, "Indeed, the machines say he died, so he must have truly died." It does not cross the mind of the reader, who is so cautious about the Bible, that John Doe's case is an index of the inadequacies of the clinical method in determining death. So I say, let the experts find us a man like Lazarus who has been dead for four *days*, and interview him, someone who was stone cold and in rigor mortis. Till then, I shall lean in the direction of Scripture.

Another thing the Bible says: you cannot any more sit at a seance and summon Uncle Rex than you can dip a fishing pole into the water at Dover, England, and pull in the same little gray fish you would if you fished in Miami. "But it looks the same." Indeed it does.

In the Gospel of Luke, Christ gives us a significant lesson.

Do not allow imagery like "Abraham's bosom" to throw you, unless you are willing to do a word study on Hebrew origins; it is a most real and apropos term. This settles the matter of the "impassable barrier." But again, do not grab onto the vehicle of the story, the imagery or the setting, to invalidate it unless you are willing to undertake the scholarship required to intelligently comprehend and critique it.

> Now there was a certain rich man, and he habitually dressed in purple and fine linen, gaily living in splendor every day. And a certain poor man named Lazarus was laid at his gate, covered with sores, and longing to be fed with the crumbs which were falling from the rich man's table; besides, even the dogs were coming and licking his sores. Now it came about that the poor man died and he was carried away by the angels to Abraham's bosom; and the rich man also died and was buried. And in Hades he lifted up his eyes, being in torment, and saw Abraham far away, and Lazarus in his bosom. And he cried out and said, "Father Abraham, have mercy on me, and send Lazarus, that he may dip the tip of his finger in water and cool off my tongue; for I am in agony in this flame." But Abraham said, "Child, remember that during your life you

> received your good things, and likewise Lazarus bad things; but now he is being comforted here, and you are in agony. And besides all this, between us and you there is a great chasm fixed, in order that those who wish to come over from here to you may not be able, and that none may cross over from there to us." And he said, "Then I beg you, Father, that you send him to my father's house—for I have five brothers—that he may warn them, lest they also come to this place of torment." But Abraham said, "They have Moses and the Prophets; let them hear them." But he said, "No, Father Abraham, but if someone goes to them from the dead, they will repent!" But he said to him, "if they do not listen to Moses and the Prophets, neither will they be persuaded if someone rises from the dead" (Luke 16:19-31, NASB).

Christ's teaching here is rich with truths, and should be read again and again. Nevertheless, the main fact for us at this point is the statement, "Between us and you there is a great chasm fixed, in order that those who wish to come over from here to you may not be able, and that none may cross over from there to us." In short, the barrier is impassable between them, not to speak of between them and the living. So who is showing up at the seances and on the Ouija boards? - - non-human spirits, as we have observed in earlier chapters.

Yet another truth emerges from the above teaching which we should not let escape us—the human condition of how men react to the truth. If men are not persuaded in their hearts by the simple truth of Scripture, "neither will they be persuaded if someone rises from the dead." This is a profound statement. Remember, hordes of people saw the Red Sea part, crossed into the wilderness with Moses, and drank from springs in the desert opened up by the staff of Moses, but later they actually renounced what they had seen in order to make and worship a golden calf at the base of Mount Sinai. The miracles did not change their hearts permanently. People are enraptured for a while, but often the feeling melts away. The truth, however, remains and is changeless.

What does God say of death? What do we learn from the hundreds of verses in the Bible?

Death is the "final enemy" to be cast into "the lake of fire," and it was the first curse. Balanced on a perfectly free decision at a particular time and place in history, death entered like an infinite garbage dump on a pellucid mountain lake. In a trice, its impact reverberated across all creation. By free will, Adam and Eve in Genesis 3 opted for the promise of knowledge "to be as a god" and, as a consequence, lost his very real kingship of this world.

The succeeding king, according to the Bible, is called "the prince of this

world" (John 12:31). The one who pulled the greatest con job ever on the two perfect people is also the author of death's entry into our domain of existence, and his name is Satan. That is what the Bible says.

Physical death has been the most apparent feature of death, and it has reigned across the centuries. But that is only the tip of the iceberg, for there is more to death than physical destruction or entropy. When the Fall occurred, more terrible was the immediate void created, the literal disfellowshipping with the living God. Our entire nature was reamed out in a moment, and we as a people were changed utterly within. We became depraved. Were God without mercy, we would have been consumed in the fire of judgment then and there (but, you see, there was this matter of the promised Messiah, Jesus Christ).

A perfect universe, as God originally made it, knows nothing of the unending wastage and agony of death and decay. Death serves no purpose in such a universe. It is contradictory to the character of the eternal, holy, and perfect God to create perfect images of himself in a physical medium, only to have them melt away into grotesque caricatures reminiscent of Dorian Gray. Remember, he who made billions of galaxies can quite capably sustain an eternal body in his creation. He can do it. But we forget this.

All we have ever known in our present experience is death reigning in a fallen universe, creation travailing in third gear. So since death is everywhere, we conclude that it must be the status quo of all existence and all conceivable existence. But God's revelation disagrees. It did not start out that way. Disbelieve if you will—because your ability to conceive of this hampers you—but that does not alter the fact that God did not make man in his image to die! God himself declares this.

The Bible speaks of three forms of death: spiritual, physical, and eternal death. "The Bible does not know the distinction, so common among us, between a physical, spiritual, and an eternal death; it has a synthetic view of death and regards it as separation from God."[4] We think of it as the cessation of existence. The Bible speaks of death as the cessation of our connection with the eternal God. Now that puts us in a new ball park. "The wages of sin is death" (Rom. 6:23).

1. Spiritual death. Our souls are cut off from God even as we live at the moment. We are born that way, and this is the condition in which a majority of people eke out their shoddy existence apart from the Messiah (Eph. 2:1, 5, 12; 4:18). They are desolate, hollow, empty, alone, afraid, willful, perverse, antagonistic, and stained in every sense of the word. This is how the Bible defines death working in our everyday lives (Gen. 6:5; Rom. 7:18). Our consciences constantly testify against us, while a general dread of punishment fills our hearts. We have guilt and are polluted. In the sight of God we are unrighteous and unholy, which is manifested in our thoughts, words, and deeds. Like an unending stream of poison invading a clear mountain spring, the soul is a battlefield of conflicting passions, thoughts, and desires. Harmony of life is destroyed, and pain is the real companion in our suffering state. Christ proclaimed that we are bondslaves of sin. This is the day to day curse of the Fall.

2. Physical death. Perhaps one of the cruelest things I could do would be to walk along a long shoreline with a corkscrew and grab one conch shell after another, pulling them out of their shells and leaving them writhing on barnacle-covered rocks, and then, with hammer and pliers, rip the shells indiscriminately off turtles and snails. The point is, to have the whole creature, we need the shell as well. Just part of it does not work.

Man is neither a bodiless spirit nor a spiritless body according to the Designer. For God to restore man after death is to make him wholly man, not just a disembodied spirit. The abnormal condition is to have the spirit ripped from its flesh. This is part of the curse of death. The ultimate state is the restoration of the whole man, which will occur on the eternal day. We wait for the memory of God to reassemble those who lived. It will happen.

Just as surely as the original models of Leonardo da Vinci's machines have been duplicated down to the last nail and wire by reading the original plans, the very God who holds the atoms in place to form a trillion crystal lattices here and so many mountains there, can do the same in reassembling we who have existed in the flesh whom he created in the first place.

That physical death is lamentable is evidenced as we see Christ at the tomb of Lazarus. "Jesus wept" (John 11:35). To have the crown of God's creation divided asunder unnaturally, the body rotting and the spirit temporarily amputated, is more of an abomination, an indignity, than it would be to have the beaches coated with de-shelled mollusks.

3. Eternal death. "This may be regarded as the culmination and completion of spiritual death. The restraints of the present fall away, and the corruption of sin has its perfect work. The full weight of the wrath of God descends on the condemned. Their separation from God, the source of life and joy, is complete, and this means death in the most awful sense of the word. Their outward condition is made to correspond with the inward state of their evil souls. They experience pangs of conscience, and physical pain. 'And the smoke of their torment goeth up for ever and ever' (Rev. 14:11)."[5]

This final state of eternal death follows the judgment on the Great Day. We do not see the last of death at somebody's funeral. That is just a stage, not the true end. When we say that death is a curse, quoting the Bible, it means literally that it is a curse. You do not wash it away any easier than you wash off burning napalm. Wake up!

Is it lightly, then, that Paul booms out with a rejoining shout, "0 death, where is thy victory? 0 death, where is thy sting?" (1 Cor. 15:55, RSV; Paul quoting Isa. 25:8). Can we fathom the deep plan of the Overcomer, and the depth of the "final enemy," death? Death tugs relentlessly, for it is intertwined in the deepest fabric of our lives.

It is no small miracle, then, for Christ to raise all of mankind, to say, "I am the resurrection and the life; he who believes in me, though he die, yet shall he live" (John 11:25, 26, RSV).

Soon after Christ uttered the above declaration into the tomb of the man who had been dead for four days, that man Lazarus emerged; he would live the remainder of his life as a normal man. The Bible does not record even a hint of some discorporated sojourn into the realm of spirits, though the opportunity was amply there if ever there were a time to do it. Instead, the Bible assures us of something else: Lazarus is to be with Christ forever; and on the eternal day, all who are "in Christ" will stand with Lazarus, not as spirits, but as resurrected, glorified creatures with bodies of immutable beauty, containing the innate power to survive for eternity.

No, our bodies will not be exactly flesh and blood; they cannot be what they are here (see 1 Cor. 15:50). For those bodies to inherit eternity, the contrast between them and our present bodies is such that we are now more like the supposed phantoms, and those eternal bodies will be the real bodies, the substantive ones. It is we who live in the land of shadows, as C.S. Lewis observed in his brilliant allegory, *The Great Divorce.* To speculate beyond the clear statements of Scripture would be folly.

Who is this One who has conquered death across the ages? Who is the real Christ? That is what I asked in a small South Indian hotel room right before I met Him and was converted. This came after two years in India as a foremost disciple of a miracle-working, self-proclaimed messiah. When I called out, two thousand years after His advent, it was Christ Himself who entered my life. I was healed in mind and spirit in a manner that no other encounter in my life has come near. I got up from my knees with a totally new orientation, a new heart, mind, and values; a sense of hope, a sense of joy. As I came to know the Scriptures in the following years, I knew why. To change a single life is a miracle. To see the record of millions of lives changed through this One, Christ, during the last two thousand years, is an undeniable miracle.

We are talking about the real Christ of Scripture, the sovereign Lord before whom "'every knee shall bow,' . . . And 'every tongue shall confess' that Jesus Christ is the Lord" (Phil. 2:10-11, Phillips). We are not talking about some so called higher master (the Bible predicts many false Christs).

The true Christ of Scripture is the Christ of history, the One foretold in 332 specific prophecies in the Old Testament. Among those prophecies are those of his nativity (Isa. 9:6); his Bethlehem birthplace (Mic. 5:2); his descent into Egypt (Hos. 11:1); the massacre of innocents (Jer. 31:15); his ministry in Galilee (Isa. 9:1,2); his rejection by the Jews (Psa. 2:1; 22:12; 41:5; 69:8)'; his persecution (Psa. 22:6; Isa. 49:7; 53:3); his betrayal for thirty pieces of silver (Zech. 11:12); and his desertion by his disciples (Zech. 13:7).

If we examine the Christ of history we have left the realm of myths. In his wake we see a world turned upside down, and the shock waves continue. The early church spilled out their lives by the tens of thousands, not for a myth, but for One who said to them, "Behold my hands and feet, that it is I myself: handle me, and see; for a spirit hath not flesh and bones, as ye see me have" (Luke 24:39). He is the One whom Job anticipated over a thousand years earlier, when he said, "I know that my redeemer liveth, and that he shall stand at the latter day upon the earth: and though after my skin worms destroy this body, yet in my flesh shall I see God" (Job 19:25, 26). More than 85 specific and fairly extensive references to bodily resurrection are in the New Testament.' It is a cornerstone of biblical Christianity, and those who argue around it are opposing the Christ of history.

Where do we tangibly see death defeated by the Christ of history? Where was his role as Savior completed? If God's greatest effort throughout history was to produce the Messiah, not by bludgeoning the world but by the most careful loving plan, the mission of Christ was crucial. Meanwhile, the opposition throughout history has seemed staggering; consider Moses riding history's course on a papyrus raft, or that single family of Noah's escaping the deluge, or Joseph and Mary fleeing into Egypt with the young Jesus. Remember, if all of the family lines across any age could have been cut off or polluted, that also would have annihilated the messianic line, made God's word untrue (an impossibility), and therefore, by history, made God un-God. Who do you think is behind this kind of deep thinking and planning?

The greatest wail in the history of mankind occurred at the cross of Christ, but it was not Christ who was wailing; it was that terrible genius, the former "illuminated one," who had played cosmic chess with God.

What happened on that hill of Golgotha overlooking Jerusalem? The debt of sin of the human race was erased, making possible reconciliation with God. If the human race had looked hopelessly lost and forever cut off from God, suddenly there was the doorway into redemption, not for a few, but for a great multitude, as was promised to Abraham.

For a moment the event on the hill looked like the destruction of God's plan, until what had really happened entered the mind of the Adversary. Then the terrible realization must have hit, akin to the defeat of Napoleon, where for an instant he owned the empires of the world as he saw the remnants of a conquered army. The next moment he looked about and, on all sides, looming on the hilltops, were the immense garrisons of the enemy. The tables had utterly turned.

This sounds simple, but it is deep. God is infinitely honest, infinitely just. Therefore, he cannot base His universe on the Truth but then mend it with lies. If a house has burned down, it has burned down. You build it again from scratch; you do not cross it off the record and say it never was there, or daydream it away. If you do, your foundations were not of truth. When a perfect man, Adam, brought sin into existence in our world, it took the exact counter payment for sin (death) of a totally perfect Man to satisfy the laws of the Creator and reverse what had happened (i.e., legitimately build another house). None but Christ has been perfect and sinless. This sinless Messiah fulfilled the prophecy in Isaiah and died to save the human race. On that cross an ultimate solution was arrived at which would mean eternal bliss for those of us who would entrust our lives to him; it means what would otherwise be impossible for us—entering fellowship with the eternal God whose brilliance pales the light of a billion suns.

A fact of history is staring us straight in the face. When they brought Christ's body down from the cross before the eyes of Israel, the people knew well the prophecy that the Messiah was to rise again. The Sanhedrin knew it, the priests knew it, and the Pharisees and Sadducees knew it, as did the common people. Caiaphas and Pontius Pilate knew it. So what was the plan? Cap the tomb with an immense boulder, seal it with the seal of state, and place a Roman temple guard in front of the tomb (they did). Then, to really drive their point home, when the three days had elapsed, their task would be simple enough: to parade the mangled corpse of Jesus through the streets of Jerusalem, that would annul Christ's claims. That would annihilate belief in Him forever. But there was the matter of an empty tomb. Suddenly a band of frightened and disconsolate men became bold. The disciples risked their own lives, for they had walked and talked with their risen Lord.

16

Conclusion

At the outset of this book, we saw in "Sudden Death" what is supposed to take place at death, according to this recent "scientific breakthrough" of Moody and Kubler-Ross. This view has taken the nation by storm. We have looked at the traditions of the psychics, mediums, and occultists; the yogis, Eastern mystics, and mystery religions; the Western thinkers, philosophers, scientists, and cosmic humanists; and finally we looked at biblical Christianity to see what Christ and the Bible really have to say about death.

Since we were aware that most of the above traditions claimed to be in allegiance with Christianity and often borrowed Christian terms, in our search we compared biblical passages with the various claims of the different traditions. At the end of our investigation we found that the Christian teaching on death is utterly unique and will not blend into these other beliefs. The ancient tradition and the biblical tradition stand opposed, and the gap between them is enormous; their views of death do not harmonize at all, but rather, are directly set against each other.

Immediately before we looked into the teachings of the psychics and mediums, we tried to find an acceptable definition for death. This brought into question whether any of Moody's subjects had in fact died at all. The case seemed to be that the machines and clinicians had mis diagnosed death, and that the experiences reported by Moody's subjects were perhaps due to other causes than death, perhaps something closer to the dream state had been approached, or some physiological event had affected them. But the pattern of their reports seemed unusual.

Looking into the world of psychics and mediums, we saw that their tradition stems from ancient occultism. Immediately we found that biblical passages sternly warn against mediumship and familiar spirits. The revelations among mediums and psychics, such as Cayce, Roberts and Van Praagh all varied along similar but confusing lines. As opposed to the prophets of the Bible, the mediums often were morally debased, hostile to God, and in the grip of a force which was clearly not altogether good. We noted a profound similarity between the modern Moody--Kubler-Ross model of death and what the psychics teach. In the candid confessions of Raphael Gasson, an ex-medium from London, we saw an explicit one-for-one correspondence between the death reports in *Life After Life* and the major tenets of the worldwide Church of Spiritualism, a connection too uncanny to be accidental. Then we discovered that Kubler-Ross herself used mediums and had her own spirit guide named Salem. Having known Moody personally, I knew he was by no means naive regarding the tenets of spiritualism, but had been a quiet seeker for years. To what did the Bible and Gasson attribute the experiences of Moody's subjects and the mediums? The deceptive powers of evil.

We considered the mystics and yogis of the East and traced many of their teachings back to ancient Babylon, where we saw the ancient priesthood, the divine-within concept, reincarnation, self-evolution, the psychic sciences such as astrology, and the idea of man becoming God. It became clear that the teachings of the psychics led directly into this view of reality. We discovered that the heart of the Eastern tradition—that the higher self is one with God—is the essence of the Genesis lie given to Adam and Eve in the Bible. The East portrayed death as a release and a dear friend, but the terrible facts of life in India today brought the fruits of this belief into question, and the biblical tradition was clearly antithetical to the Eastern view.

Turning to the West, we saw a Western world in an identity crisis. The West was ready to leap from the philosophy of "scientism" right into mysticism, without a second thought. As we peered into the past to look at the foundations of Western philosophy, we saw what had happened. Centuries ago, in the name of objective truth, God and the Bible had been thrown out the window, leaving a large gap in man's soul. Existentialism and despair grew as a mood. But there were still large questions, which science and rationalism and the philosophies after rationalism had not answered, and man's world had become no better. Man, believing in the Kantian notion that no unified field of knowledge connecting the physical with the spiritual was possible, became desperate and started to look for any convenient doorways to escape the constant hum of existential despair. That opened the doors for Tim Leary, the gurus, psychedelia and the new mystics. The setting in our culture became ideal for the reception of the new "scientific breakthrough" concerning death offered by Moody and Kubler-Ross.

Finally, as many are beginning to do today, we turned to the Bible. Science and philosophy have in no way been able to dispose of the Bible. Upon investigation, it turns out to be the most incredible book on earth. God's powerful words say that death is not a dear old friend, but an ancient enemy, and that there is but a single escape from the curse of death: Jesus Christ. The alternative is truly terrible.

After considering the Bible, it became even more clear that not one of the other traditions truly accepts the biblical view of death without redefining concepts and terms and then squeezing them through a special filtering system. The Bible's potent, startling, frightening, and potentially hopeful statements about death have been blurred, if not obliterated, by the other traditions. Those traditions have disposed of the transcendent, holy, and personal God of the Bible while shifting the balances of good, evil, and morality. They also have deftly disposed of the most threatening thought for all mankind: hell, about which the Bible warns both compassionately and sternly. But in expunging hell, they also have jettisoned eternal heaven, with its immensity, bliss, and grandeur.

What do we say now about driving a car and fantasizing a death experience, as in "Sudden Death"? In the end, this breakthrough by Moody and Kubler-Ross to solve the riddle of death offers little more than a trifling, phantasmagoric, palisades park alternative to the biblical heaven. The imagery they give does not need to be caricatured; it serves as its own bleak caricature, with its pastel colors, amorphous forms, and smoky encounters. Even without the biblical perspective to guide us, to see death painted with such saccharin benignity, winking at us behind a honeycomb smile, has too much of the chilling effect of a "setup" to really be convincing. Something does not feel right underneath the reassuring background melodies, the reception-room smiles, and the clinical aerosol fragrance. One still gets the feeling that something foreboding is behind the door of the Moody--Kubler-Ross reception office, some terrible machination reminiscent of the Frankenstein story.

Who are these beings of light with their effervescent cheerfulness? When unmasked, what are these "old friends" like? I believe we would discover the very thing Moody and Kubler-Ross are most quick to dismiss: that the being of light was among the legions of "wicked potentates" and "cosmic powers of evil" that the Apostle Paul refers to in Ephesians 6. Make no mistake, the only possible biblical explanation for these beings of light is that they are demons masquerading as angels of light.

Since we are now opening a spiritual "can of worms," I will mention a brilliantly written book entitled *Hostage to the Devil*, which deals with the subject of demonic possession.[1] Steeped in mature and deep insight, it was written by Malachi Martin, the one-time religion editor of *The National Review* and a former professor and Oxford scholar. It is based on contemporary accounts, two of which are entitled "The Rooster and the Tortoise" and "Father Bones and Mr. Natch." One is about a man who until recently was a famous parapsychologist. The subtle and sweet quality of some of these spirit deceptions is awesome considering how grotesque they become when the game is up and they are unmasked.

At this point, it is time to discuss the heart of the issue. Satan is no myth, despite his aptitude at mythologizing himself behind numerous respectable academic arguments and ethnic cliches. He is only too real and is a terrible, dark strength. The Bible states that as his time draws to a close, his campaign of deception will be pervasive, subtle, and ruthless. He is described as resembling a roaring lion out to devour the souls of men (see 1 Pet. 5:8). He hates Christ, and he hates you and me. As the supreme genius of deception, he can use almost anything to achieve his end: myths, pipe dreams, fashionable philosophies of the day, literary poignancies, distractions, religions, psychic powers, gods, legends, and anything else which can act as a wedge between us and Christ. He even uses the computer and economics to gather power over human souls. Finally, he uses such palatable models of death as we encountered in "Sudden Death" to sweeten its bitter taste and drug our minds. He does this using a fair-minded, unbiased, benign, and humanitarian voice.

This adversary is a fleeting blemish compared with God, whose Grace and Love is beyond measure. The adversary is parasitic on goodness, yet as a deceiver he has done untold damage.

Whether or not the individual has a love of the truth in the end is maybe even *the* critical factor in finding the grace of God. When we discover that Christ is who He said He is, the true messiah, then we can face the great divide under his power and covering with no fear. If we are in Him, the riddle of the ages is solved. We enter by the doorway of grace.

So consider very soberly the immensity of your choice and its consequences as you decide what you really believe is the surest and safest way to navigate the great divide. As for me, I will throw my life in with Him who gave his life for us, the very Lord whom I once met in a South Indian Hotel room when I called upon Him in absolute desperation. He changed my life from that point on and is our final hope in entering the gateway of death.

Notes

The New Breakthrough

1. Raymond A. Moody, Jr., *Life After Life* (Covington, Ga.: Mockingbird Books, 1975), p. 9. Used by permission. Copyright © Mockingbird Books, Covington, Ga., 1975. All rights reserved.

2. Ibid., p. 23.

3. Ibid., p. 79.

4. Ibid., p. 84.

Finding a Definition for Death

1. John Weldon and Zola Levitt, *Is There Life After Death?* (Irvine, Calif.: Harvest House, 1977], p. 32.

2. Ibid.

3. Ibid., p. 37.

4. Ibid., p. 38.

5. Raymond A. Moody, Jr., *Life After Life* (Covington, Ga.: Mockingbird Books, 1975), p. 103.

6. Elisabeth Kubler-Ross, interview in *National Enquirer* (Feb. 1, 1977). 7. Deccan *Herald* (Dehli, India, Oct. 26, 1977).

Breakthroughs of the Spirit World

1. Thomas Sugrue, *There Is A River* (New York: Holt. Rinehart & Winston, 1942], p. 361.

2. Ford also gave Sun Myung Moon, head of the Unification Church, a number of seances. On May 13, 1964, Ford's spirit guide, Fletcher, said of Moon, "He is a child of the new age—the Aquarian age. He has tremendous spiritual power and also psychic power . . . he is a prophet" (Allen Spraggett, *Arthur Ford: The Man Who Talked with the Dead* New York: Signet Books, 1974], p. 271). Copyright © 1973 by Allen Spraggett. Reprinted by arrangement with The New American Library, Inc., New York, N.Y.

3. Joseph Bayly, *What About Horoscopes?* (Elgin, Ill.: D.C. Cook, 1970), p. 63.

4. Spraggett, p. 25.

5. Ibid., p. 41.

6. Ibid., pp. 130-31.

7. Ibid., p. 125.

8. Elisabeth Kubler-Ross, interview in the *National Enquirer* (Feb. 1, 1977).

9. Spraggett, p. 270.

10. Raphael Gasson, *The Challenging Counterfeit* (Plainfield, N.J.: Logos, 1966), p. 48.

11. Spraggett, p. 210.

12. Gasson. p. 54. (The identical beliefs come through Moody's editorializing; see p. 70 of his book.)

13. Ibid., p. 119.

14. Ibid

Beings of Light or False Angels of Light?

1. James Pearre, interview with Elisabeth Kubler-Ross, San Francisco *Examiner* and *Chronicle*, Nov. 14, 1976. Reprinted, courtesy of *The* Chicago Tribune.

2. Raymond Moody, *Life After Life* (Covington, Ga.: Mockingbird Books.

1975), pp. 72-73.

3. Ibid., p. 45.

4. Ibid., p. 66.

5. Ibid., p. 70.

6. Ibid.

7. Ibid.

8. Ibid., italics added.

9. Jane Roberts, *Seth Speaks* (New York: Bantam Books, 1973).

10. Jane Roberts, *The Seth Material* (New York: Bantam Books, 1970).

SpiritVoices: James Van Praagh

People OnLine

2 James Van Praagh *Talking To Heaven: A Medium's Message Of Life After Death* (NY: E.P. Dutton) p. 54.

3 David Klinghoffer, "Ghost Story," *National Review*, April 6, 1998

4 Jon Carroll, *Van Praagh's Friendly Ghosts*, Salon Magazine, April 17, 1998.

5 April 22, 1998 10:19 p.m. EDT http://www.nando.net

6 Op sit Jon Carroll.

7 Raphael Gasson, *The Challenging Counterfeit* (Plainfield, N.J.: Logos, 1966), p. 48.

8 Allen Spraggett, *Arthur Ford: The* Man *Who Talked with the* Dead (New York: Signet Books, 1974) p. 210

Gary Zukav's Seat of the Soul

1 Zukav, Gary, *The Seat of the Soul,* (NY, NY, Simon and Schuster, Fireside, 1990). p. 239.

2 p. 34.

3 p. 122.

4 p. 135.

5 p. 171.

6 p. 172

7 p. 143

8 p. 144

9 p. 111

10 p. 153.

11 p. 43.

12 p. 41.

13 p. 43.

14 p. 45.

15 p. 37

16 p. 176.

17 p. 178.

18 p. 175

19 p. 197

20 p. 198.

21 p. 180

22 p. 114

23 p. 115.

24 p. 106

25 p. 111

26 p. 186

27 p. 126

28 p. 125.

29 p. 126

30 p. 162

31 p. 162

32 p. 162

33 p. 137

34 p. 239.

The Ancient Tradition

1. C.S. Lewis, *Miracles* (New York: Macmillan, 1947), pp. 84-85.
2. Erwin Schrodinger, *My View of the World* (London: Cambridge U. Press, 1964), p. 67.
3. That such a created substrate has existed seems a reasonable inference from the account of Genesis 1:1-10, where it is revealed that the initial stage of cosmic formation was a state which possessed true created existence, but was "formless and void." It was only later that this unitary state of bare existence was molded by God to pass through the primordial duality (the separation of light and darkness, v. 4) and beyond into increasingly elaborate dualizations (separation of firmaments, land from water, etc., vv. 6-27) by means of which God built up the complex forms of material creation.

Dying in India

1. Tal Brooke, *The Amazing Advent* (New Delhi: Nabajiban Press, 1971].
2. The *Bhagavad Gita*, 7:14.
3. Ibid., 8:6.
4. Ibid., 8:9, 10.
5. Tal Brooke, *Avatar of Night*.

Death in Babylon

1. Elisabeth Kubler-Ross, *Death:* The Final *State of* Growth (Englewood Cliffs, N.J.: Prentice-Hall, 1975), pp. 1-3. © 1975. Reprinted by permission of Prentice-Hall, Inc., Englewood Cliffs, N.J.
2. Brooks Alexander, "The Coming World Religion," an essay published by Spiritual Counterfeits Projects, Inc., Berkeley, CA. Used by permission.
3. Alexander Hislop, The Two Babylons (Neptune, N.J.: Loiseaux, 1916), pp. 20, 78, 96, italics added.
4. Manglwadi, The World of Gurus (New Delhi: Vikas Publishing, 1977), p. 174, italics added.
5. Kubler-Ross, pp. 164-67, italics added.
6. Lennie Kronish, "Elisabeth Kubler-Ross: Messenger of Love," Yoga *Journal* (Nov.-Dec. 1976).

The Present Mood

1. *The Daily Progress* (Nov. 25, 1977), Charlottesville, Virginia.
2. For a more thorough analysis of the historical progress/on, refer to the Appendixes by

Robert Schlagal.

The Death of God

1. C.S. Lewis, *Mere Christianity* (New York: Macmillan, 1952), p. 32.
2. Malcolm Muggeridge, as quoted in *Eternity* (April 1972).

The Eternal Word

1. F.F. Bruce, *The Books and the Parchments* (Old Tappan, N.J.: Revell, 1963), p. 88. Used by permission.
2. Josh McDowell, *Evidence That Demands a Verdict* (Arrowhead Springs, San Bernadino, CaIff.: Campus Crusade, 1972), p. 19. Used by permission.
3. Reprinted by Baker Book House, Grand Rapids, 1965.
4. J.N.D. Anderson, "The Resurrection of Jesus Christ," *Christianity* Today (March 29, 1968).
5. A.T. Robertson, as quoted by McDowell, p. 46.
6. Sir Frederic G. Kenyon, as quoted by McDowell, p. 47. 7. McDowell, p. 150.
8. Norman L. Geisler and William E. Nix, *A General Introduction to the Bible* (Chicago: Moody, 1968), p. 263.
9. Clark Pinnock, *Set Forth Your Case* (Chicago: Moody, 1971), p. 86.
10. C.S. Lewis, *Mere Christianity* (New York: Macmillan, 1952), p. 40.

The Eternal Day

1. C.S. Lewis, *Screwtape Proposes a Toast* (London: Collins, 1965), p. 109.
2. The Westminster Confession, chap. 32.
3. Ibid., chap. 33.
4. Louis Berkhof, *Systematic Theology* (Grand Rapids: Eerdmans, 1941), p. 259. Used by permission.
5. Ibid., p. 261.
6. E.W. Hengstenburg, *The Christology of the Old Testament* (Grand Rapids: Kregel, 1970).
7. See James Strong, *The Exhaustive Concordance of the Bible* (New York: Abingdon, 1958 reprint).

Conclusion

1. Malachi Martin, *Hostage to the Devil* (New York: Bantam Books, 1977).

Appendix I

1. William Barrett, *Irrational Man* (Garden City, N.Y.: Doubleday, Anchor Books, 1958), pp. 216-17.
2. Ibid., p. 217.
3. Ernst Cassirer, *The Philosophy of the Enlightenment* (Princeton, N.J.:
Princeton Univ. Press, 1951), pp. 13, 14, italics added.
4. Ibid.

5. The thinking of Kant quite naturally led to Kierkegaard and from there to modern existential theology, in terms of which God is not an active, intelligent, and sovereign Lord, but a creative life force, a symbol of wholeness or resolution, or a value-producing agent which can only be encountered inwardly in subjective experience. For all intents and purposes in this camp, the God of Scripture is dead.

End Run Publishing

"To provide an end run"

The publishing giants keep producing books that fit within certain narrowly prescribed politically correct & secularist views, thus keeping from publication books that challenge their views, regardless of how well written. Free speech is thus effectively defeated at the editorial & marketing gateways of these 70-story monoliths. Today's high-tech revolution—digital short run printing, powerful computers, & the Internet—may eventually level the playing field (How many publishing giants started as humble two room bookbinders in Brooklyn at the turn of the century?). Stay tuned for more titles.

Tal Brooke has written numerous books on diverse subjects. His most popular book in the West, *When The World Will Be As One,* was a 100,000-copy bestseller marketed to a very limited audience. He has written seven other books, including *Riders of The Cosmic Circuit,* which came out in Europe. Keep your eyes out for these and other titles being considered.

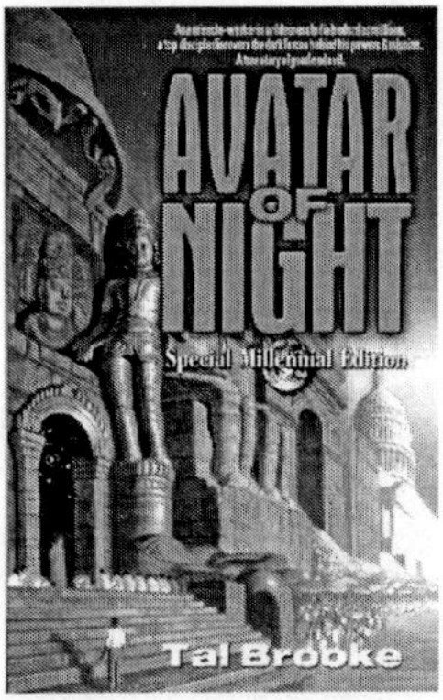

Tal Brooke, President of SCP, is on the Web at the SCP Web Site: http://www.scp-inc.org/
Check out the in-depth Journals and Newsletters that SCP (Spiritual Counterfeits Project) has published over the years.
Or phone the SCP offices at: 510-540-0300

END RUN PUBLISHING
1442A WALNUT STREET, PMB 387, BERKELEY, CA, 94709

Avatar of Night, The Millennial Edition by Tal Brooke

The Indian Bestseller was released in December of 1999 and is the most complete version ever published.

As Woodstock and the Apollo moon landing lit up the skies of history, Tal Brooke flew to New Delhi, quickly becoming immersed in the vast subcontinent of India as he pursued a radical pilgrimage of consciousness. After quickly exhausting the 'Grand Tour' of landmarks popularized by the spiritual tourists of the West, Brooke plunged into wilderness India, and the journey shifted into high gear.

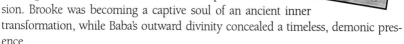

From their first meeting, Brooke was heralded by Sai Baba, India's greatest miracle-working godman, as the inner-circle disciple who, like Oppenheimer at Los Alamos, would help trigger the explosion of India's ancient mystical tradition into the Western world. Within Baba's enchanted realm, Brooke saw and experienced things that seemed to obliterate all Western conceptions of reality as his journey vectored further into an alien universe. What had appeared as the prized state of godlike enlightenment, which seemed just within reach, became a precipice—not of enlightenment—but obliteration, even possession. Brooke was becoming a captive soul of an ancient inner transformation, while Baba's outward divinity concealed a timeless, demonic presence.

After two years of surrender to a Being who claimed to be God on earth, something remarkable happened. The end-game of spiritual powers ensnaring one man's soul turned abruptly and miraculously. Poised on the edge of a precipice, Brooke was rescued from above.

With hauntingly vivid images, unexpected humor, and a profound passion for truth, Brooke lays bare the powerful reality of good and evil and of things beyond the familiar realm of the senses, in a book that will not be easily forgotten.